Executive Leadership

A Manual for the Principles of Supervision

by
NATHAN AXELROD

Bobbs-Merrill Educational Publishing
Indianapolis

Copyright © 1969 by Flower Lane Publishing Co., Inc.
Printed in the United States of America
All rights reserved. No part of this book shall be
reproduced or transmitted in any form or by any means,
electronic or mechanical, including photocopying, recording,
or by any information or retrieval system, without written
permission from the Publisher:

        The Bobbs-Merrill Company, Inc.
        4300 West 62nd Street
        Indianapolis, Indiana 46268

First Edition
Sixth Printing—1979
ISBN 0-672-96054-0 (pbk.)

Table of Contents

PREFACE	ix
INTRODUCTION	1
SECTION ONE –	
SOME FUNDAMENTAL CONCEPTS OF SUPERVISION	3
CHAPTER ONE –	
FUNDAMENTAL CONCEPTS	5
SUPERVISION	5
LEADERSHIP	6
ORGANIZATIONAL STRUCTURE	7
HUMAN RELATIONS	12
EFFECTIVE COMMUNICATIONS	14

SECTION TWO –
THE SUPERVISOR AND THE EMPLOYMENT FUNCTION 19

CHAPTER TWO –
EMPLOYMENT SYSTEMS 21

THE CENTRALIZED EMPLOYMENT SYSTEM 22
THE DECENTRALIZED EMPLOYMENT SYSTEM 23
THE COMBINATION EMPLOYMENT SYSTEM 24

CHAPTER THREE –
EMPLOYEE RECRUITMENT – LABOR RESOURCES 25

DIRECT APPLICANTS 26
NEWSPAPER ADVERTISEMENTS 26
PLACEMENT BUREAUS 30
REFERRALS 31
RADIO AND/OR TV 31
THE PROSPECT FILE 31

CHAPTER FOUR –
EMPLOYEE SELECTION 33

THE APPLICATION BLANK 34
THE INTERVIEW 34
TESTING 38
EMPLOYMENT PROCEDURES 39

SECTION THREE –
THE SUPERVISOR AND THE TRAINING FUNCTION 43

CHAPTER FIVE —
    TRAINING SYSTEMS   45

CHAPTER SIX —
    TRAINING THE NEW EMPLOYEE — INITIAL TRAINING   49

CHAPTER SEVEN —
    THE SPONSOR SYSTEM   53

    THE SPONSOR'S ROLES   55
    CRITERIA FOR SELECTING SPONSORS   56
    THE SPONSOR'S RESPONSIBILITIES   57
    FINE POINTS IN SPONSORING   57
    REWARDING THE SPONSOR   58

CHAPTER EIGHT —
    FOLLOW-UP TRAINING FOR ALL EMPLOYEES   61

CHAPTER NINE —
    EXECUTIVE TRAINING   65

    EXECUTIVE RECRUITMENT   66
    HOW SUPERVISORS ARE TRAINED   69

SECTION FOUR —
TRAINING TECHNIQUES   75

CHAPTER TEN —
    CONDUCTING A DEPARTMENT MEETING   77

CHAPTER ELEVEN —
    THE CONFERENCE METHOD   85

    CONFERENCE PROCEDURE   88

SECTION FIVE —
SUPERVISORY PRINCIPLES AND TECHNIQUES   97

    CHAPTER TWELVE —
        ROLE-PLAYING   99

        HISTORY AND BACKGROUND   100
        FORMS OF ROLE-PLAYING   100
        USES OF ROLL-PLAYING IN SUPERVISION   101
        THE "MECHANICS" OF ROLE-PLAYING   102

    CHAPTER THIRTEEN —
        J.I.T. — JOB INSTRUCTOR TRAINING   111

        WHO NEEDS TO USE J.I.T.?   111
        HISTORY AND DEVELOPMENT OF J.I.T.   112
        J.I.T. TODAY   113
        SOME SIMPLE SEMANTICS   113
        HOW J.I.T. WORKS   114
        SUMMARY   122

    CHAPTER FOURTEEN —
        EMPLOYEE EVALUATION   123

        WHAT IS EMPLOYEE EVALUATION?   124
        WHY EVALUATE?   125

WHO SHOULD EVALUATE?	127
WHEN TO EVALUATE	128
HOW TO EVALUATE	128
THE RATING INTERVIEW	137

CHAPTER FIFTEEN —
GIVING ORDERS — 145

WHAT TO CONSIDER IN GIVING ORDERS	145
WAYS OF GIVING ORDERS	147
WRITTEN ORDERS	150

CHAPTER SIXTEEN —
MAINTAINING DISCIPLINE — 153

THE REPRIMAND	163
THE CORRECTIVE INTERVIEW	165

CHAPTER SEVENTEEN —
HANDLING COMPLAINTS AND GRIEVANCES — 169

CHAPTER EIGHTEEN —
THE SUPERVISOR AND FREQUENT, LONG-RANGE PROBLEMS — 175

RUMORS	176
ABSENTEEISM	179
FAMILIARITY AND FRATERNIZATION	180
COLLECTIONS	184

ALCOHOLISM 186
OLDER WORKERS 188

BIBLIOGRAPHY 191

Preface

For almost two decades, my colleagues in the junior/community college field, as well as those connected with schools of business at a number of universities, have joined my friends in the personnel and training areas of the New York marketing scene in a continuous request: "When are you going to write that book?" They mean, of course, this manual for the Workshop in Executive Leadership.

"There is nothing in print for *us* in *our* field," they have complained. "Practically everything written on principles of supervision has a heavy industrial/plant personnel management background. We want something for the student or junior executive in the merchandising, advertising, business management field." The greatest demand, however, has come from our students here at the Fashion Institute of Technology because they are required to take the Executive Leadership course and they willingly do so. Their complaint has had much merit and justification — they have had reading assignments in bits and pieces of as many as twelve texts.

But the real credit for pushing me into this impossible task must go to my newly found publisher, Mr. Donald Sheff, President of Flower Lane Publishing Company, a subsidiary of ITT. His wily probing, after "Selected Cases in Fashion Marketing" had gone to press, uncovered the need for this book. His subsequent guile and blandishments did the rest — produced the manuscript that has been locked in my thoughts, on scraps of paper, and on dozens of mimeographed handouts for so many years. And as this goes to press, the publishing fever has really gotten to me; I am already planning a new and enlarged edition for 1971.

Nathan Axelrod
Fashion Institute of Technology

New York, New York
August 1968

Introduction

As the subtitle may indicate, this is a text for the student who hopes to be an executive in the marketing field which includes such broad areas of business enterprise as merchandising, advertising, and retailing. It will also be useful for the junior executive or trainee already in these fields.

"Business" students, unlike their liberal arts contemporaries, know pretty well that they want to join the ranks of management in the not-so-distant future. "Executive Leadership" hopes to help them achieve their goal by creating a guidebook that will chart their course.

The course in Executive Leadership has four principal objectives:

> **1.** To enable the student to understand the importance of leadership in business and to develop basic leadership skills and abilities.

2. To teach the basic principles of supervising people in the day-to-day job of getting work done through people.

3. To acquaint the student with the various ways of teaching people to do their regular tasks.

4. To give the student an insight into human relationships so he is able to work well with others.

Section I

Some Fundamental Concepts of Supervision

Chapter One

Fundamental Concepts

SUPERVISION

Supervision has been defined in many ways but the simplest definition is the best one: *"Supervision is getting work done through people."*

The Supervisor is an employee who has been given authority to direct the work of others. The Supervisor, in turn, has the responsibility for their work or output. His own job has been defined and established by the company as part of the company's table of organization. Thus, the Supervisor may be at the first level of management, such as a Department Manager or assistant buyer, where he is directly concerned with a specific group of employees; or he may be a middle management Supervisor where he deals with and supervises first-line Supervisors – e.g., a buyer who supervises several assistant buyers.

Since all supervisory positions are not alike, we must think of supervision not in terms of one definite kind of job, but in terms of a broad category of supervisory positions. Generally, the Supervisor's job begins with his selection of the right person for the right job or task. The Supervisor's job involves getting that person motivated or interested in doing that job well, teaching or training the employee how to do the job; and, if necessary, correcting the employee and the job performance; at regular intervals he must effectively measure that performance; he must give praise when due and reward the employee over the longterm; and finally, where necessary, he must transfer or dismiss the employee when such action is required. These are the complex and interesting jobs of supervisory people.

LEADERSHIP

In theory and in practice, *supervision* has become synonymous with *leadership.* It is easy to see how and why this has happened. It is rather difficult to picture a Supervisor who does not have to possess leadership qualities, characterstics, and traits that are most desirable.

The student in an Executive Leadership course such as this naturally has a keen interest in learning what makes for good leadership ability, and therefore for good prospective Supervisors. Such students are living testimony to the fact that the cliche, "Leaders are born, not made," is inherently false. The Executive Training programs in both college and industry have shown that educated and intelligent young people with the *desire* to become Managers, can acquire the necessary *skills* and techniques in a classroom by studying the principles and methods of supervision. These will be discussed in detail in the chapters that follow.

There have been many studies made to determine what

qualities are essential or important for success as a leader/Supervisor. A vital factor in developing effective leadership is helping the executive trainee to acquire or to bring out already-present desirable qualities. A quick look at the common traits desirable in good Supervisors includes:

1. Enthusiasm and alertness
2. Tact
3. Patience
4. Ability to get along with others
5. Ability and willingness to communicate
6. Ability to plan and organize thoroughly
7. Decisiveness
8. Realism
9. Fairness and impartiality
10. Initiative

This is a simple, incomplete, yet formidable list. But these personal qualities help to determine whether or not the leader/Supervisor can stimulate and encourage a group of people to do an effective job.

ORGANIZATIONAL STRUCTURE

In defining supervision, reference was made at the beginning of this chapter to "the company's table of organization." All well-organized business firms have a clearly defined chart which shows each specific position in relation to the over-all structure. This organization chart also establishes the lines of authority which help to fix *who* is responsible for *what*. It is also helpful in showing *where* and to *whom* certain responsibilities and authority have been delegated by a higher authority. In other words, a senior-management person delegates a part of his responsibilities to a middle-management person, who in turn delegates or divides parts of this responsibility among the first-line Supervisors under his supervision. If each delegation of responsibility is to be both meaningful and workable, however, it is necessary to give each level of supervision a measure of authority. "Responsibility without authority breeds anarchy and chaos," is a very accurate statement.

This concept of authority and responsibility will be of particular interest to the future young merchandising executive. While many other forms of business enterprise have long been accustomed to working under the carefully delineated lines of an organization chart, this has been a relatively modern concept in merchandising organizations. As a result, there frequently exists a general air of confusion in mercantile organizations, especially in the large department store.

In 1927, Paul M. Mazur, now the senior partner in one of the nation's most influential investment firms on Wall Street, proposed an organizational structure plan as a guide for use by department stores to supplant the poor or nonexistent ones in vogue at the time. The Mazur Plan, as it became known, came after a long study and was intended to supply an urgent need. Briefly, it proposed that a large store be set up or organized into four major divisions — Merchandising, Sales Promotion, Control, and Management. The following simplified chart shows these four divisions, each based upon one of the major functions of the business.

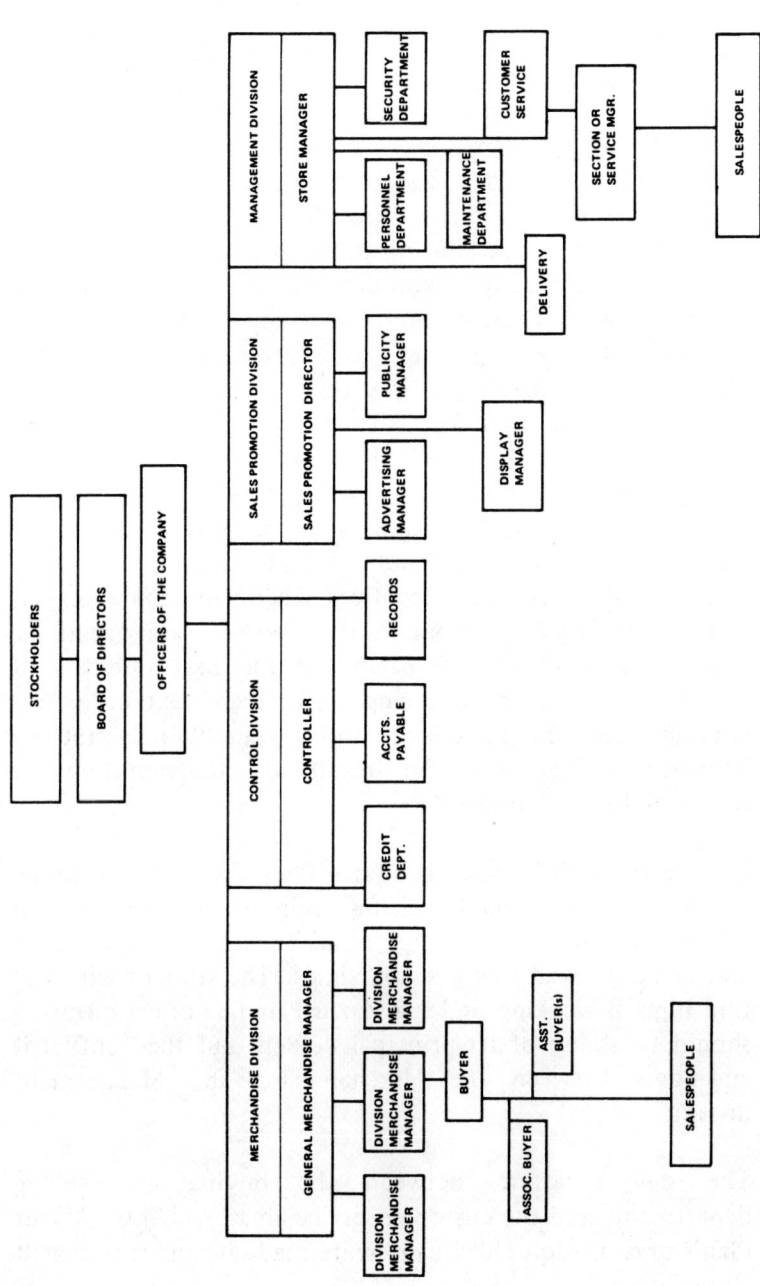

As the chart indicates, each division specializes in an important aspect of the store's functions. Each is essential to the whole organization. The chart clearly defines the authority of each division, and sets up its responsibilities. While the Mazur Plan was a definite improvement over existing plans and while it provided a blueprint for those firms without a real organization chart, it had one clear failing: the salespeople who formed the backbone of the organization were under the control of two different major divisions. On the one hand, each buyer, as the head of a Merchandise Department, was responsible for sales in his department and, therefore, the salespeople came under his direct supervision. On the other hand, a Service or Section Manager who reported to the Management Division, which had no direct interest in sales or merchandising, controlled many of the salespeople activities involved in "customer service." These service executives scheduled such things as the sales force's lunch hours, shifts, days off, and vacations, and could move people around in the best interests of customer service. Not knowing where their next order was coming from, the salespeople were generally in a state of confusion. This was the result of the mixture of responsibility and authority.

Despite this major fault, the Mazur Plan was the first genuine attempt in the merchandising field to provide a real organization plan. Many large retail organizations still use it and are organized along similar lines. The student who will find himself working under a Mazur Plan line of organization should be aware of its principal defects and the conflict it engenders between the Merchandising and Management divisions.

The daily warfare between the buying and selling departments and the customer service areas, which the Mazur Plan's organization chart can create made it apparent that it must be remedied to prevent real trouble. Accordingly, the National Retail Merchants Association (N.R.M.A.), the parent-body of the nation's retail industry, ordered an intensive study by a well known industrial management engineering firm. Several years ago, their plan for department store organization, revising the Mazur Plan, was unveiled. The following is a simplified version of the principal ideas contained in that report.

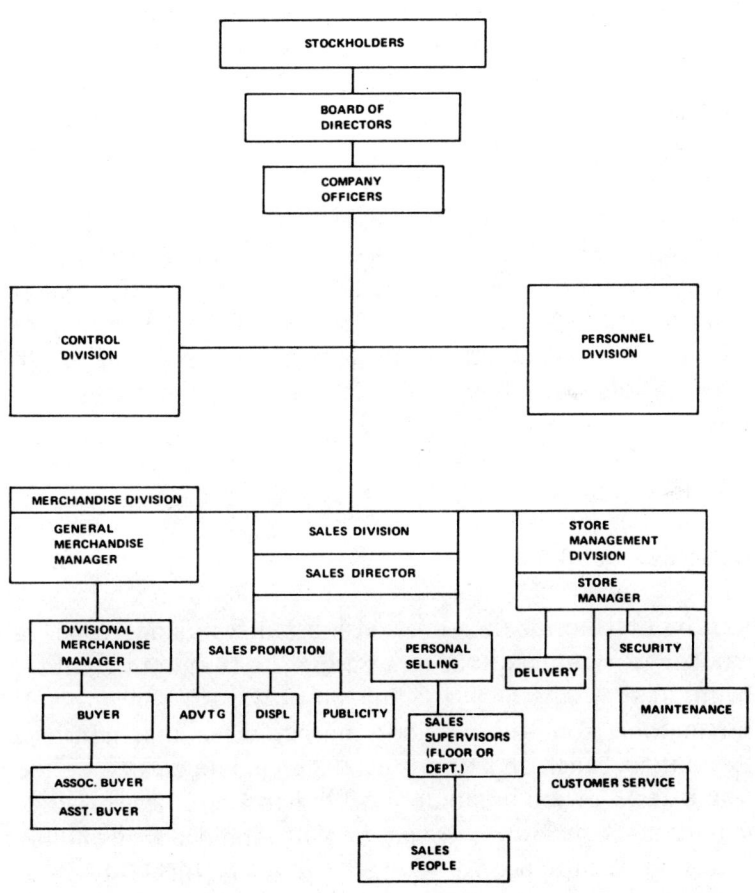

It is evident from a study of this organization chart that several new and interesting factors are involved. The most important factor is that there is no longer the split control over salespeople. The creation of a personal sales structure eliminates any conflict and confusion about to whom the salespeople report. Another departure is the creation of a "line and staff" organization plan in place of the old "line" organization created by the Mazur Plan. This means that there will no longer be four equally important divisions all allegedly involved in buying and selling when in fact, they all are not. Instead, the Control or Finance Division and the Personnel Division (which formerly worked under the store Management Division), have become "staff" organizations – assisting and serving all the "line" divisions – those divisions which are actually concerned with buying and selling activities.

It is interesting that while some of the leading stores have already seen the advantages of the new plan, the movement away from the Mazur Plan has been quite slow. The student should be aware that the problems evolving from organizational structures will greatly affect his own work and future in the merchandising field.

HUMAN RELATIONS

Supervisor-subordinate relationships have undergone a number of significant changes during the twentieth century. In the first two decades, the Supervisor was still the autocrat, a hangover from the previous century when the Industrial Revolution began and flourished. The climate created by the fear of loss of job or home was used to keep the worker in line. The Supervisor/autocrat had life-and-death economic power over his people, and he used it ruthlessly. The inevitable result was the growth of unions despite every legal device that was used by employers to prevent their formation. In the years following the first world war, including the boom-and-bust period of the late 20's and early 30's, the labor unions began to make themselves felt as a force to be reckoned with by management. They received their "Magna Charta" during the early days of the New Deal under the N.R.A. (National Recovery Act), and finally, the Wagner Act. As labor unions and government laws and regulations put the pressure on management, a human relations approach became an important factor which Managers found played a large role in getting more and better work done through people.

Millions of words have been written about "human relations" in the past 20 or 25 years. In addition to hundreds of books, there have been untold articles in professional, learned, and popular journals on this topic. The sociologist and the industrial psychologist have made it their property. The relatively new behavioral sciences have embraced it. Yet, it is possible to state the fundamental law of the human relations approach to supervision in one simple phrase that is based on one of mankind's oldest adages: "Do unto others as you would have them do unto you." In the language of the Supervisor — "Treat others as you want to be treated yourself."

It is as simple as that. It is not a social reform movement, as some sociologists have inferred. It is not a benevolent autocracy or paternalistic form of supervision where management has humanely decided to be nice to their people. It is, instead, a common sense, cash register approach to an old problem of how to handle people on the job. Treat workers tactfully, nicely, courteously, kindly, etc., and they will respond in kind — by producing more. The machine operator will turn out more pieces and the salesperson will sell more merchandise. Just like that! It all goes back to one of the most basic human drives — the desire to feel secure, the desire to be wanted. A feeling of insecurity engendered by poor supervisory tactics of brusqueness, rudeness and fear, causes production (sales) to go down. The Supervisor who treats his co-workers as he himself would like to be treated is saying to his subordinates by his actions and words: "We want you, we need you, we are a team working together." Every action, every word of the Supervisor who is aware of the human relations approach reflects this attitude and is in turn reflected by the rank-and-file worker.

EFFECTIVE COMMUNICATIONS

As in the case of human relations, there are very few topics that arouse Managers more than, "communications." Again, hundreds of books and millions of words have appeared in periodicals on the topic. Each year conferences, seminars, and workshops are held under different auspices. Many colleges give courses, and some even offer an entire cirriculum, in "communications." It is a matter of common agreement by many Supervisors that communication is the most pressing problem of present-day management.

Incidentally, the human relations approach to supervision is one of the key reasons for much of this concern with effective communication. In order for good human relations to exist, there must be effective communication between Supervisor and staff. Several other factors that have influenced the focus on the need for better communications include the growth of unions both in size and in economic, political and social power. In addition, employees (and people, generally) are more and more independent in their thinking and their ways, they are demanding and getting more democratic action in all phases of their lives, including their work situations. Finally, there is the great increase of education on all levels in the past several decades — both formal education and education received through the communicative arts, such as television and radio.

It is for the above-mentioned reasons, and for many others, that agreement is general in management circles that there is a need for more and better communication on the job.

Since it would take several good-sized volumes to set down the important facts on this subject, it seems necessary to limit this topic to the following important aspects:

1. What is to be communicated

2. How it should be communicated

3. Factors that assist in communication

4. Factors that hinder communication

1. **What is to be Communicated**

    a. Of course, in light of present-day conditions, the most important aspect of communication includes those things that the rank-and-file employee wishes to have as much knowledge as possible about: wages, hours, benefits, vacations, rules and regulations, company policies, etc. The employee also has need to know such things as the organizational structure of the company, who his Supervisors are, how grievances are handled, the company's sales or products, merchandise information, and the many other operational facts too numerous to enumerate.

    b. On the other hand, the Supervisor and the firm are

required to know as much as possible about each employee; including his skills, aptitudes, ambitions or ability to advance, any suggestions the employee may have, any grievances or worries about the job or the company, etc.

2. How it Should be Communicated

There are a number of commonly used means or forms of communication which the Supervisor and/or the company may use:

a. Signs or posters.

b. Bulletin boards.

c. Meetings — formal and informal.

d. Verbal announcements by the Supervisor; loudspeaker announcements by the company.

e. The suggestion system.

f. The house organ (company magazine or paper).

g. The mail (letters and memoranda) — both intra- and interdepartment mail, as well as the United States mails.

h. Employee handbooks and manuals.

3. Factors That Assist in Communication

Up to this point, this section has dealt with communication on the large, company-wide basis. This, and the next sub-section (4) deals with personal factors involved in communication. Some of the needed elements for good communication between Supervisor and Subordinate include:

a. The Supervisor, in and by his communicating, must sound as well as be sincere.

b. In the communication, the spirit of human relations in which the dignity of the employee is upheld at all times must prevail. In other words, the communication must not talk *down* to the recipient.

c. There is an important need for the Supervisor in planning and executing his communications to be concerned with and have a real understanding of his staff — their motives, their attitudes and their opinions.

d. The Supervisor should encourage his subordinates to express themselves on how they feel about matters pertaining to the department, not only to bring things that bother them out into the open, but also to establish a good climate for future communications.

e. The Supervisor must *"sell"* himself and his ideas to those he supervises. He must plan his communications logically, as a salesman plans his sales talk. He must also be persuasive in order to convince his staff, just as the salesman must secure conviction in order to close the sales.

4. **Factors That Hinder Communication**

It is also important for the Supervisor to know what to

avoid in communicating so that a knowledge of these negative factors which interfere with effective communication on the job may be prevented or, at least, diminished.

a. The Supervisor in attempting to be sincere should avoid being too smart-alecky, or too sharp in his words or actions.

b. The Supervisor should be careful of the choice of his language to be sure that those who are due to receive the communication can understand the message fully.

c. The Supervisor must avoid any words or actions that indicate animosity or bias against any individual group, class, race, color, creed, educational background, etc.

d. In his efforts to *"sell"* his ideas, the Supervisor must not use gimmicks, devices or obvious techniques so that those who receive his persuasive effort feel that he is trying to trick them.

Thus, it can be seen that communication brings many responsibilities to the Department Head. Since it is necessary for the Supervisor to get his work done through his people by communicating with them, effective communication has become his most important job.

Recommended Reading

Dooher and Marquis: Effective Communication on the Job — pp. 13-23, 35-53

Halsey, G. D.: Supervising People — Chapter 18

Section II

The Supervisor and the Employment Function

Chapter Two

Employment Systems

It is expected that any executive in a firm should have a general knowledge of how each division and/or department in his firm is organized and how it operates. The department that he heads or is a part of will, of course, be most familiar to him. As indicated in the previous chapter, one of the major departments of any fair-sized organization is concerned with the personnel function, and the Supervisor probably will have to work more closely with this department than any other except his own. Because of this major consideration, we will first examine the *employment* aspect of personnel, and then in a subsequent section, the *training* phase of personnel. In addition, there is a strong possibility that the junior executive may find himself in a situation where a first-hand knowledge of the employment process becomes very important to him in the day-to-day operation of his department. This will become apparent when we examine the three types of employment systems into which most employment departments fall.

1. THE CENTRALIZED EMPLOYMENT SYSTEM

There is little doubt that the *Centralized Employment System* is the predominant one in current American business practice. Under this system, the Employment Department of the Personnel Division of the company has the sole authority to recruit, screen, test, interview, select, and place the applicant in the job that is available in any department of the firm. While the job order may originate from the Department Head, the Employment Department independently and without consultation, delivers the new employee to the Supervisor *after* the employment process is completed.

REQUEST FOR EMPLOYEE			
DATE REQUESTED	DEPARTMENT		
NUMBER NEEDED	MALE or FEMALE		PART or FULL TIME
AGE	PERMANENT or TEMPORARY		OVERTIME
DUTIES (BE SPECIFIC)			
EXPERIENCE DESIRED			
DATE NEEDED	REQUESTED BY		APPROVED BY

FORM 568D 2500 8-43L

In many cases the new employee first undergoes a period of training for several days or more in a Centralized Training Department before being introduced to the Supervisor and his new department.

2. THE DECENTRALIZED EMPLOYMENT SYSTEM

The Centralized Employment System seems to prevail in a majority of the larger business organizations of the country. But there are a sufficient number of firms that operate under a Decentralized Employment System to warrant a cursory examination of this method. The Decentralized Employment System is generally found in smaller business organizations; it is also quite prevalent in many resident buying offices, in many central buying offices of chains, and in many individual stores of a chain where the store Manager exercises the personnel function as one of his many duties.

Under a Decentralized Employment System, there are often no personnel or employment offices involved; or where such a company function does exist, it is of a minor nature. It is each Department Head's responsibility to carry out the employment process of recruiting, screening, testing, interviewing, selecting and placing the new employee in his own department.

Obviously this decentralized approach adds an additional burden to the already overworked typical Supervisor. This means that he will either delegate this responsibility to his assistant or to some other "qualified" subordinate. Where he cannot or will not delegate the employment function, the Department Supervisor tries to do the job himself and very frequently the normal operating problems force him to push his employment responsibilities aside or to do a perfunctory job. One can safely say that much of the inefficiency and the terribly expensive high labor turnover that some firms experience is due to the hasty and poor selection of employees as a result of the haphazard manner in which the overburdened

Department Head is forced to work.

3. THE COMBINATION EMPLOYMENT SYSTEM

A compromise method which combines the diametrically opposed Centralized and Decentralized Employment systems has made itself felt in recent years. Under the combination method, the Employment Department of the Personnel Division retains the responsibility for recruiting, screening, testing, and preliminary interviewing. Once the Employment Office determines that it has one or more qualified applicants, the Department Head comes into the picture. The prospective employee is either interviewed by the Department Head on the premises of the Employment Office, or the applicant is conducted to the Department Supervisor's area for an in-depth interview. The essence of the combination method is that the Department Supervisor makes the final determination whether or not the applicants presented by the Employment Office are to be hired. If the Department Head does not feel that the candidates are qualified, he may reject them and the employment process is begun all over again by the Employment Department.

Recommended Reading (see Chapter 4)

Chapter Three

Employee Recruitment – Labor Resources

If the junior executive finds himself employed in an organization which adheres rigidly to the Centralized Employment System described in the previous chapter, he will have little or nothing to do with the employment process. Thus the material to be presented in this and the subsequent chapter will be of limited direct value. The indirect value of this information will be great, however, since it is important for any executive to understand how the *entire* organization operates and how departments and divisions interrelate. Obviously, if you find yourself working for an organization in which the Decentralized System or the combination method is in use, you will find the information that follows to be particularly important and practical.

The first *actual* step in the employment function is securing and maintaining an adequate and efficient labor force. Thus, the Supervisor will find that he or his duly delegated representative must make a study to determine which of the standard sources of labor supply are best suited to his needs.

He should next select several good sources in each category of labor resources and carefully cultivate them so that he will readily be able to fill any employment need as it arises. The following are some of the principal sources of labor supply that the Supervisor can attempt to develop:

DIRECT APPLICANTS

Research in this field has indicated that this is probably the most important source of labor. People will go, for example, directly to the store looking for a potential job now or for the near future; or they will act impulsively upon a long-felt idea and inquire about job possibilities while they are shopping in the store or its immediate environs. A recent survey by a large store in the metropolitan area of one of the country's largest cities conclusively showed that a very sizable portion of the store's applicants came into the Employment Office carrying packages purchased in that store. Of course, we must recognize one important factor: to attract good individuals to seek employment, your firm must be known in the community as a good place to work. This can only be accomplished by raising and maintaining high employee morale by a carefully planned and executed employee benefit plan together with a good human relations program.

NEWSPAPER ADVERTISEMENTS

Frequently, it will be necessary to use newspaper advertisements as a means of recruiting help. The Manager should keep records on the responses to such advertisements to help him determine which papers in his area are the best for this purpose. In most cases, the use of newspaper advertising will be restricted to attempting to fill jobs that require special technical skills or knowledge, and to recruiting workers at peak periods when labor is hard to get. If the

Manager uses this medium, he should be sure that the advertisement is well-worded and that it is the proper type of advertisement for the position involved. In general, ads may be divided into two major categories:

1. **Classified Advertisements** are found in one specific section of the newspaper and are generally quite regidly categorized as to position by alphabetical order.

Classified advertisements may either be *"open"* — inserted over the store's name — or *"closed"* or *"blind,"* in which the store's identity is concealed by the use of a box number. The blind advertisement is used to screen applicants or to prevent hurting employee morale.

2. **Display Advertisements** are those which are found scattered throughout the newspaper, such as the regular merchandise-for-sale ads.

Merchandise Controller

This position, with a leading men's & women's apparel manufacturer, requires experience in coordination of sales forecasting, production planning and inventory level controls. Must be skilled in development and use of statistical controls. We are looking for a thoroughly qualified individual. Salary commensurate with experience; liberal benefit program.

REPLY IN CONFIDENCE TO:

Executive Conference Leader

Major New York City Department Store is looking for experienced conference leader to conduct Middle Management Training and Work Simplification Programs. College Graduate with experience in education or industrial training required. Liberal benefits. Please send resume including education, work experience and salary desired.

Retail Chain

PRODUCT SERVICE TRAINING MANAGER

Major national retail chain requires addition to staff in expanding Service Department. Outstanding opportunity for qualified man with background in white and brown goods—who can accept responsibility for planning, developing and conducting service training in field operations, on corporate basis. Require 8-10 years experience in technical service. Excellent income potential.

Please send complete resume indicating present income level to

Employment Manager
An Equal Opportunity Employer

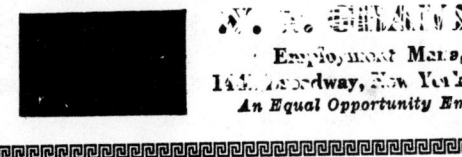

Display ads may be used either for important or "scarce" skilled or executive positions or for large numbers of rank-and-file employees for peak period hiring.

Newspaper advertising is an effective method of securing help if it is properly prepared and strategically used. Too frequently, however, time and money are wasted by hit-or-miss advertising. Planning is what counts.

PLACEMENT BUREAUS

Placement bureaus are frequently good sources of applicants, particularly in larger population areas. The Manager whose business is located where there are no such agencies would do well to make contacts with some in larger cities.

Employment agencies may be classified into two distinct categories:

1. **Free placement bureaus** are conducted by different public, social service, fraternal, religious, philanthropic, and educational organizations. These include the many offices maintained by the various state employment services; the placement bureaus of high schools, business schools and colleges, as well as the bureaus maintained by churches, the national fraternal orders, and other national social service agencies.

    In general, the free placement agencies are good sources of labor supply for lower echelon or non-executive positions, except for the college offices which are excellent resources for the Executive Training Program.

2. **Private employment agencies** are a well-established source of labor supply. In some cases they charge the applicant a fee for securing a position for him; in other cases, especially in the placement of executives, it is customary for the company to pay this fee. Most reliable executive placement agencies make it a practice to guarantee their placements for one year where the firm pays the fee.

    As a rule, firms do not use privately-owned agencies to fill regular positions, but reserve this resource for skilled employees, trainees, and executives. The well-run employment agency generally performs a highly selective service for the supervisor in screening and preliminary interviewing.

REFERRALS

Referrals are another labor resource. These are people who come to the company seeking positions on the *recommendation* of current employees, vendors or their salesmen, customers, or important civic or business people in the firm's trading area. Of all the foregoing, current employees' referrals are probably the best since it is unlikely that employees of regular standing would jeopardize their own positions by recommending anyone undesirable. But these referrals can also be a source of embarrassment to the Supervisor because those making such recommendations frequently give the applicant the feeling that their name will open the door to employment without fail. Thus, if referrals are to be developed into an important source of labor supply, the Manager must make it quite clear at the very beginning that the final hiring decision belongs to him alone. Once this is understood, the firm will have put referrals on the same basis as other standard labor sources.

RADIO AND/OR TV

Radio and/or TV can be used as a means of recruiting labor for peak periods or special events in the same manner as large classified or display advertising. This applies, of course, only to those areas where radio or TV rates are comparable to newspaper rates in coverage and cost.

THE PROSPECT FILE

The prospect file or *waiting list* can be developed into one of the company's top sources of labor supply. It has been placed last on this list not because it is the least important but because the waiting list is composed of people who have made a good impression on the Supervisor from any of the above-mentioned sources. Therefore, if at the time of application there are no positions open, the Manager should still interview the applicant carefully and make detailed notes on the application form — notes that will be meaningful at some future time. The names of good former employees whose reasons for separation in the past are valid can readily be added to this group of new candidates. All these names are kept in job categories such as stock people, cashiers, salespeople, etc., until vacancies occur. The prospect file, carefully compiled and carefully used, can go a long way towards meeting the regular employment needs.

Recommended Reading (see Chapter 4)

Chapter Four

Employee Selection

The next and very important consideration in the Supervisor's attempts to secure the right person for the right job is to set up simple procedures to insure the proper selection of a good staff for his department. After the Manager has used the best-suited labor resources described in the previous chapter, it is quite probable that several applicants will soon be available; then the employment process will continue on its way.

Incidentally, in the retail field it is important that the Supervisor be constantly aware that every applicant is an actual or potential customer. While he may not be in a position to offer too many jobs in his department to those who apply, the Manager must, accordingly, give each prospective employee prompt and courteous attention. If the Manager is engaged when the applicant arrives, he should be treated like any waiting customer: be recognized, invited to sit down, and told that he or she will be seen very shortly.

THE APPLICATION BLANK

When the Supervisor is free, the first order of business should be to give the applicant a chance to fill out an application blank (see page 35). Even if the candidate is quite obviously someone the Supervisor would not employ, the applicant should be given an opportunity to complete the blank, but should be told frankly at this time that there is no opening. This rejection must be handled courteously and kindly. There is nothing more devastating to the morale of a person out of work than to be treated shabbily by an employer.

THE INTERVIEW

The physical space where the interview will take place needs some thought and planning. Every department has some area or office where privacy is assured. It is the height of poor taste, for example, to interview an applicant on the working floor within the sight and hearing of customers and other employees. If at all possible, the place used should be quiet and free from disturbances. Effective interviewing is only possible when both the applicant and the interviewer are at ease. A nice office makes a favorable impression on the applicant and sets the tone for a good interview.

The actual interview, in which the Supervisor is face-to-face with the prospective employee, is the most important portion of the entire employment procedure. Out of a friendly discussion between the applicant and the interviewer comes the Manager's decision to offer the applicant a position, as well as the applicant's determination to accept or reject that offer. For a successful interview, the first task of the Supervisor is to put the prospective employee at ease. Most people who are job hunting tend to be tense; they look upon the interview as an ordeal. If the interviewer makes it his business to establish this as a friendly

APPLICATION FOR EMPLOYMENT

EMPLOYEE'S N° _____
STORE STAMP

SOCIAL SECURITY NO. _____
DRAFT CLASSIFICATION _____
DATE CLASSIFIED _____

NAME (LAST) _____ (FIRST) _____ (MIDDLE) _____ MAIDEN NAME _____
PRINT NAME

ADDRESS _____
NUMBER   STREET   CITY   ZONE NO.   STATE

PHONE NUMBER _____   DATE OF BIRTH _____   ARE YOU A CITIZEN OF THE U.S. _____

MALE _____ FEMALE _____   WEIGHT _____ HEIGHT _____   SINGLE, MARRIED, DIVORCED, WIDOWED, SEPARATED? _____   WITH WHOM DO YOU LIVE? _____

CHILDREN _____ OTHER DEPENDENTS _____   WHAT IS YOUR HUSBAND'S BUSINESS? _____   WHAT IS YOUR FATHER'S BUSINESS? _____

ANY RELATIVES OR FRIENDS WORKING FOR _____?   IF SO, GIVE NAME AND POSITION _____

WHAT IS THE STATE OF YOUR HEALTH? _____   HAVE YOU ANY PHYSICAL DEFECTS? _____   GIVE DETAILS _____

POSITION DESIRED _____   DO YOU WANT FULL TIME? _____ PART TIME? _____   HAVE YOU EVER WORKED FOR _____   IF SO WHEN? _____

EDUCATION

	GRADUATED YES / NO	IF NOT GIVE NO. OF YRS. COMPLETED	NAME OF COLLEGE - DEGREES
GRADE SCHOOL			
HIGH SCHOOL			
COLLEGE			
SPECIAL TRAINING			

PERSONAL REFERENCES
(DO NOT GIVE RELATIVES)

NAME	NAME
ADDRESS	ADDRESS
OCCUPATION	OCCUPATION
PERIOD OF ACQUAINTANCE	PERIOD OF ACQUAINTANCE

RECORD OF PREVIOUS EMPLOYMENT

NAME AND ADDRESS OF LAST EMPLOYER	KIND OF BUSINESS AND WHAT WAS YOUR POSITION?	WORKED UNDER WHOM? REASON FOR LEAVING	HOW LONG WERE YOU EMPLOYED FROM / TO	WHAT WAS YOUR SALARY?
NAME AND ADDRESS OF NEXT TO LAST EMPLOYER	KIND OF BUSINESS AND WHAT WAS YOUR POSITION?	WORKED UNDER WHOM? REASON FOR LEAVING	HOW LONG WERE YOU EMPLOYED FROM / TO	WHAT WAS YOUR SALARY?
NAME AND ADDRESS OF PREVIOUS EMPLOYER	KIND OF BUSINESS AND WHAT WAS YOUR POSITION?	WORKED UNDER WHOM? REASON FOR LEAVING	HOW LONG WERE YOU EMPLOYED FROM / TO	WHAT WAS YOUR SALARY?

I AGREE, IF EMPLOYED, TO CONFORM TO ALL THE RULES OF THE EMPLOYER. MY EMPLOYMENT MAY BE TERMINATED AT ANY TIME AT THE OPTION OF THE EMPLOYER OR AT MY OPTION WITHOUT NOTICE AND WITHOUT ANY CAUSE THEREFOR AND IN SUCH EVENT I SHALL ONLY BE ENTITLED TO COMPENSATION FOR THE TIME I HAVE ACTUALLY WORKED.

DATE _____ 19___ SIGNATURE _____ WITNESSED BY _____

conversation between two people, it will be a rewarding experience. The Supervisor's friendliness will encourage the applicant to talk freely about himself. In this way, additional information can be secured to fill the gaps in the application blank.

Every interview is different, of course, and it is not easy to set up rigid criteria for the interviewing process. However, the following guideposts can be used to measure the average applicant:

1. **Appearance**: The total picture should convey an impression of neatness and intelligence. It is also imperative that the applicant be in obvious good health.

2. **Attitude**: The Manager must come to the unmistakable conclusion that the applicant is alert, enthusiastic, imaginative, and really interested, in a positive way, in finding the right kind of job.

3. **Speech**: Since many employees must meet the public, good speech, and the ability to express oneself clearly and in a pleasing voice are most important.

4. **Experience**: If experience is a prerequisite for the position open, the interviewer should obtain the candidate's background by some direct questions based on the application blank's information.

5. **Education**: Most firms today require a minimum of a high school education or its equivalent for consideration as a potential employee. However, there may be lower as well as higher-echelon positions which either do not require any

minimum education or can demand a college degree or even graduate school completion. The Supervisor must use his discretion in determining this qualification.

6. **Handwriting**: Many positions include the need for a neat, legible handwriting as a qualification for employment.

7. **Personality**: Because people have to work or deal with other people (customers, etc.), the applicant's manifested personality traits must be considered. The Supervisor's education, experience, and "maturity" will stand him in good stead in determining whether the applicant will "fit" in the department.

The employment interview has been called the heart of the employment process. Using the seven guideposts listed above plus any others that are pertinent to the particular position under discussion, the interviewer/Manager will be in a good position during the interview to *get* information from the applicant which will enable him to best judge the applicant's reliability, capability, and stability. But the interviewer must also *give* information to the prospective employee. Such information is frequently necessary to help the candidate decide whether or not the job is for him. Some of the facts that the applicant should be told include:

1. **Salary**: Starting salary; automatic wage progressions and/or merit raises, and their frequency; overtime pay; pay dates; and bonuses.

2. **Work Schedules**: Number of hours and specified days of work, days off; holidays; and shifts.

3. **Benefits:** Welfare or fringe benefits such as insurance, hospitalization, pensions, vacations, discounts, etc.; and extracurricular activities.

4. **Duties:** What the job entails and what is expected of him, generally and specifically.

5. **Rules and Regulations:** A very brief enumeration of any rules that might deter the applicant from accepting the position, such as no smoking or no parking facilities, etc.

6. **Promotion Possibilities:** Both to higher positions and higher wages.

7. Any other good or bad points about the job, department, or firm.

TESTING

Psychological tests offer no short-cut to the problem of finding the right man for the job; they are not tools for the amateur — which is how the ordinary Supervisor must be classified. A great deal has been written and said about the use of tests in relation to selecting employees. Some personnel authorities feel that if properly and cautiously used, psychological tests can be of help in selection and placement decisions. Other personnel people feel that the more you know about testing, the more careful and cautious you generally become in its use and the values you attach to it. One thing is certain: the Department Manager who feels that testing is the magic formula for solving all employee selection problem will soon find he is sadly mistaken. Testing, even when done by qualified experts, is of limited value and can be really misleading to the Supervisor; it is quite difficult to establish the true validity of the tests in relation to his own company. The great danger in using tests is in the taking of scores too seriously by unqualified and untrained testers. It must be remembered that tests only play one small part in the employee selection process.

There are additional drawbacks in psychological testing from the applicant's point of view. Most people tend to be apprehensive about taking tests, associating them with their school careers. And even though the employment interviewer may explain that the tests are only a part of the entire selection process, there is a tendency for the candidate to feel that his future depends almost entirely on the test results. Even if this is not really true, a critical, tense climate has been created.

Of course, practical testing for typists, stenographers, drivers, bookkeepers, and other personnel are always in order. The Supervisor would do well to have such tests for such prospective employees available at all times.

EMPLOYMENT PROCEDURES

When the Supervisor has finally decided to hire an applicant, there are a number of employment procedures that should or must be followed:

1. **Physical Examination** — Too few Managers now feel that a medical examination by a local doctor should be part of the employment process. The writer strongly feels that this is a mistake; it is a small expense that is well worth incurring. Obviously, there are certain illnesses or weaknesses or past medical histories that should readily bar some applicants from employment.

The person whose name appears below has
applied to us for a position, and has
referred us to you.
Any information furnished will be held in
strict confidence. A self addressed, stamped
envelope is enclosed for your reply.

      Yours very truly,

Name_____ Ref. #_____
Social Security No._____
Employed From_____ To_____
Position Held _____
Honesty_____
Reason for Leaving_____
_____
_____
_____
Remarks_____
_____
_____
_____
_____
    Signed_____
     per_____
H.F. 331

2. **Tax Forms** — All employees must complete an Employee's Withholding Tax Form for the collection of Federal income taxes. This is also true in those states and cities which now have a similar income tax system. These forms usually include information needed for Social Security taxes.

3. **Reference Checking** — A leading personnel authority once facetiously remarked that the only references worthwhile considering are the poor ones. While there is some measure of truth in these words, most firms will still find it profitable to check the new employee's past employment, education, and/or personal (character) references. In some cases, it will be advisable to send reference check letters immediately, to verify the information given by the applicant. However, recent surveys have shown that the use of telephone calls to the former Manager will get much more reliable and useful information. Many Supervisors will be able to give more and better information by a friendly telephone conversation, when they would normally be reluctant or unable to answer a letter. Note should be made here that the immediate Supervisor's name be obtained from your applicant; the Personnel Department or Payroll Office to which reference checking letters are normally referred are apt to be too vague about their answers. See sample on page 40.

4. **Working Papers** — If young people are being processed, working papers must be secured by them with the store's assistance. The age limit requirements for such work permits as well as "continuation school" or similar educational prerequisites naturally will vary from state to state.

The Manager must keep himself up-to-date on these regulations as they affect his area.

5. **Bonding** – The alert Supervisor will be quite aware of the need for fidelity bonding insurance, especially for those employees who have direct access to cash or valuable merchandise.

Recommended Reading

Dooher and Marquis: Effective Communication on the Job – Chapter 7

Flippo: Principles of Personnel Management – pp. 159-167, 177-197, 198-219

Halsey, G. D.: Supervising People – Chapter 7

Section III

The Supervisor and the Training Function

Chapter Five

Training Systems

The work of the Supervisor as indicated in Chapter One may be divided into two parts: the Supervisor as a trainer (teacher); and the Supervisor in his role as a Manager or as an executive. This section will be concerned with that part of the supervisory job which deals with the training of people.

TRAINING SYSTEMS

In order to understand his place in the training setup or organization of any company, the Supervisor should have a general knowledge or background of training and training systems per se.

Methods of training may be classified or categorized in a number of ways. In this chapter, we shall endeavor to examine the general aspects of training, as well as specific training programs within these broad categories. Training can accordingly be divided into three major areas:

1. Centralized Training
2. Decentralized Training
3. Combination

1. Centralized Training

In this system all of the training functions are placed under the control of a Training Department which is headed by a Training Director. The Training Department is usually an integral part of the Personnel Division. The Training Department has the task of devising and maintaining various training programs for all levels of employees. A wide variety of methods such as centralized classroom procedures, training manuals, and audiovisual aids can be effectively used in training. It should be noted that the Centralized Training System usually gives generalized training information that applies to all employees.

2. Decentralized Training

Under this system, the Department Supervisor has the full responsibility of training all the people under his jurisdiction. He has the task of devising and maintaining the training program or he may delegate all or part of this responsibility to one or more of his subordinates. Decentralized training is sometimes called on-the-job training because of the lack of a centralized training department's classroom facilities, equipment, and the specialists whose only job is training.

3. Combination

There are also some organizations where the training

function is divided between a relatively small Training Department and the Department Supervisor. In other words, this system combines some of the features of centralized and decentralized training. For example, one of the nation's largest vertical textile organizations, United Merchants and Manufacturers (U. M. & M.), has a centralized Personnel Division which hires all clerical employees for their many subsidiary companies. Then, after the employment process is completed, the new clerical employee is sent to a centralized training class where he is subjected to an orientation program and taught basic clerical skills. When the training program is over, the clerical is referred to a specific department in one of the companies where the Department Supervisor or his duly designated representative give the newcomer specific training in his own job as well as any necessary departmental information.

Recommended Reading (see Chapter 9)

Chapter Six

Training the New Employee – Initial Training

We have discussed training from the viewpoint of those with whom responsibility for training lies. Another way of looking at the training function centers on the people to be trained. Employees who need training can be grouped in several ways; but the simplest and currently most popular method is to discuss training from the viewpoint of (1) new employees, (2) regular employees, (3) executive training – for the job ahead.

As we saw in the previous chapter, new employees may be trained either in a Centralized Training System, a Decentralized Training System, or by a combination of both. In many large organizations, the combination method is prevalent. When someone is employed, his first few days in the new position are spent in a centralized training classroom situation where, together with other new employees of the company, he is exposed to a regular curriculum which might include some of the following topics:

a. **Basic systems and procedures** — in the case of a large retail store, this could include sales check writing, cash register operation, charge account procedures, etc.

b. **Rules and regulations** — basic company standards of conduct which could include dress regulations, attendance, punctuality, discounts, etc.

c. **Company policies** — basic company principles around which the business has been built and upon which the company now stands. This could include such topics as sales, advertising, refunds, delivery policies, etc.

d. **A general orientation** — about the company, including its history and development, current status, and future plans for growth. Regional or civic participation might be included here as well as any other information of which the company is proud and which could cause the new employee to feel this pride.

e. **Promotional possibilities** — growth on the job as well as within the organization.

f. **Specific information** — on company benefits, welfare plans, and company-sponsored extracurricular activities, such as insurance plans, vacations, pensions, holidays, discounts, clubs, teams, etc.

In the event that the company does not have a centralized classroom operation to handle the above-mentioned initial training program, it becomes the Department Supervisor's responsibility to see that the new employee gets all necessary information.

After the new employee has finished his initial training procedures, someone in the Employment Division of the

SALES TRAINING SCHEDULE

NAME		POSITION	SALES NO.
YOUR DEPT.	FLOOR	STARTING TIME	STARTING DATE
YOUR BUYER		YOUR ASSISTANT BUYER	
YOUR SERVICE MANAGER		YOUR SPONSOR	
YOUR FLOOR SUPERINTENDENT		YOUR DEPARTMENT MANAGER	

FIRST DAY

9:15 A.M.	Report for Training (9th Floor)
9:30	Orientation and Tour
12:00	Sales System
1:00 P.M.	Lunch
2:00	Sales System
4:15	Salesmanship
5:45	End of First Day's Training

SECOND DAY

9:15 A.M.	Report to Sponsor in Selling Department
11:00	Salesmanship (Bring Item of Mdse.)
1:00 P.M.	Lunch With Sponsor
2:00	Sales System
5:45	End of Second Day's Training

THIRD DAY

9:15 A.M.	Salesmanship (Bring another Item of Mdse.)
11:00	Sales System
1:00 P.M.	Lunch
2:00	Sales System
4:00	Training Completed, Report to Service Manager in Selling Department.

BA 630A-R

Personnel Department conducts him to his newly-assigned department and introduces him to the Department Manager whose job it is to complete this preliminary training. This situation will, of course, vary from organization to organization and from industry to industry, but basically, the employee is trained on-the-job by the Supervisor or by some subordinate designated by the Supervisor for that function. At this time, the new employee is given specific job information relating to the department and to his own position there. For example, if this were a retail store, the new salesperson would receive extensive training in the merchandise: resources, construction, care and uses, selling points, price lines, stock-keeping and any modifications of systems and procedures already learned in centralized training.

Recommended Reading (see Chapter 9)

Chapter Seven

The Sponsor System

This phase of initial training, the specific on-the-job aspect just described in Chapter Six, may best be handled, as it is in many large organizations, by the establishment of a *Sponsor System*. Under the Sponsor System, the Department Head carefully selects one or more experienced, rank-and-file members of the department to whom he delegates the authority and the responsibility for "breaking in" the new person. It must be made clear at the outset that the Sponsor is an ordinary member of the department whose chief duty is to perform the normal functions of her job. Thus, a Sponsor can be a regular salesperson whose chief job it is to sell or a cashier whose principal task is to handle money, etc. Usually it is only when there is a newcomer to be trained that the Sponsor assumes this additional function.

SPONSOR JOB PERFORMANCE CHECK LIST

NAME OF EMPLOYEE _____ DEPT. _____

General Information:

DID YOU: YES   NO

1. Introduce new employee to salespeople & insp-wrapper? ☐ ☐
2. Explain where to place **Hastes** and **Charge Hold-Overs**? ☐ ☐
3. Show employee where tallies, gift envelopes and bank check stickers are kept? ☐ ☐
4. Show employee location of telephones and directories, including Charge Authorization card? ☐ ☐
5. Point out location of fitting rooms, alteration desk, hold bars and reserve stock room? ☐ ☐
6. Show employee physical lay-out of entire floor? ☐ ☐

Stock Information:

DID YOU EXPLAIN:

1. How stock is arranged? ☐ ☐
2. The different price tags and labels? ☐ ☐
3. How to get merchandise that is not in reserve stock room? ☐ ☐
4. How to fold or handle merchandise? ☐ ☐
5. Merchandise in each stock section as to:
   - Type of Fabric ☐ ☐
   - Workmanship ☐ ☐
   - Style Features ☐ ☐
   - Washability ☐ ☐
   - Wearability ☐ ☐

System Information:

DID YOU EXPLAIN USE OF:

1. "Interdepartment" Salescheck ☐ ☐
2. Deposit Book ☐ ☐
3. Special Order Book ☐ ☐
4. "As Per" List ☐ ☐
5. Transfer Card ☐ ☐

Did you make a daily spot-check of saleschecks and tally envs.? ☐ ☐

Follow Through:

DID YOU:

1. Assist employee with first stock assignment? ☐ ☐
2. Spot-check employee's selling techniques and give constructive suggestions? ☐ ☐
3. Discuss employee's progress with Section Manager? ☐ ☐

SUBMITTED BY _____

THE SPONSOR'S ROLES

Since most Supervisors have such multi-faceted positions requiring their attention in so many different directions, training the newcomer on-the-job should definitely be delegated to a Sponsor. However, in order to select the right person for this responsible job, the Supervisor needs to establish certain criteria in his mind which will make his selection successful. To do this correctly, the Manager would do well to analyze the Sponsor's roles so that he can find the right person to fit this position. The Sponsor's many activities fall into three major categories:

1. **He is a host** who makes the newcomer feel welcome, introduces him to his co-workers and his other Supervisors, and does everything within his power to make him feel at ease and at home on his new job. The first few hours, or even the first days, are generally quite a strain on the new employee as he seeks to impress the Supervisor with his ability and to make a place for himself with his co-workers. Anything the Sponsor can do to make the newcomer feel secure is a plus factor in this regard.

2. **He is a teacher** who gives the new employee specific instructions about his job such as merchandise facts, special systems, and procedures needed on that job. He reviews the firm's rules, regulations, policies, benefits, etc., even though the employee may have attended training sessions in a Centralized Training Department. He teaches him any basic skills needed for the job.

3. **He is a supervisor** who corrects errors before they become bad habits during this learning period. He carefully follows up to keep the new employee "on his toes" until he is well able to take care of himself.

CRITERIA FOR SELECTING SPONSORS

If the Supervisor has a firm knowledge and complete understanding of the three roles that the Sponsor plays, he can now establish in his mind the criteria necessary for the selection of such Sponsors. Generally speaking, it has been found that the most effective Sponsors have the following characteristics:

1. The Sponsor is *enthusiastic* about his organization, his department, his job, and his prospects for the future. If the Sponsor is a salesperson, for example, he would be enthusiastic about the merchandise he sells.

2. The Sponsor is a *friendly* person who likes and understands people.

3. The Sponsor is a person who has both the *willingness* and the *ability* to communicate (teach) to others the basic information needed on the job.

4. The Sponsor is both *patient* and *tactful* realizing that starting a new job is a difficult thing for anyone.

5. The Sponsor is *loyal* to his company, to his department and to his Supervisor. It is quite apparent that the Sponsor is in a critical position; and he can "make" or "break" the new employee's career by his loyalty or lack of it.

6. The Sponsor is *knowledgeable;* he has sufficient experience in the company and the department to have a thorough background for the job that he is to teach. It should be noted here, therefore, that the selection of a Sponsor does not depend on seniority in the department. A person who has all of the foregoing

attributes can often make a better Sponsor than the person with the longest employment record who is lacking in one or more of these characteristics.

THE SPONSOR'S RESPONSIBILITIES

It is the Supervisor's responsibility, after selecting the Sponsor, to be sure that the Sponsor is carefully trained and completely aware of all areas of his specific job instructions. This means, for example, that if we are dealing with a Sponsor for a Sales Department, the Supervisor should prepare a checklist for the Sponsor (see Figure 10) which will cover all of the Sponsor's duties as a host, teacher, and supervisor. In the case of this sales Sponsor, the checklist would include many items under the main heading of merchandise information; there would be other items arising out of stockkeeping duties, systems and procedures, etc.

In addition to the Supervisor's responsibility for providing the Sponsor with a checklist of his training activities, many companies also provide a Sponsor's manual which pinpoints the Sponsor's duties. By devoting the opening portion of the manual to telling the Sponsor how and why he was selected for this important position, it attempts to motivate him to do a better job.

FINE POINTS IN SPONSORING

Alert and intelligent Managers are quick to agree that there is a need to find additional fine points in order to make the Sponsor System as effective as possible and to help make the new employee's training period as happy and meaningful as possible. What can be done in this respect will vary greatly with the organization and what it stands for, the region in which it is located, and similar factors. One commonly used "fine point" whose aim is to make the new employee's first day on the job as pleasant as possible under normally trying circumstances, is arranging for the Sponsor to invite the newcomer as his guest for lunch with the company picking up the tab. Another frequently used device is to have the Sponsor also extend an invitation to the new person to accompany him on his coffee break and to "treat" him to some light refreshments at company expense. In terms of building the new employee's morale and giving him a feeling that he is not only welcome but that he is wanted these efforts will surely bring results worth far more then the small cost entailed.

REWARDING THE SPONSOR

We have spent a good deal of time analyzing the job of the Sponsor and what he can do for the company and the department to which he is assigned. It makes good sense, therefore, to consider how the company can show the Sponsor its appreciation for all his efforts on its behalf. Much of a discussion on this point might seem unnecessary but surprisingly enough a recent national survey of the largest department stores in the country indicated that the great majority of the stores made little or no effort to compensate or reward the Sponsor in any way at all! These companies felt this way because they believed that the Sponsor's time belonged to the firm and that it was not necessary to pay additional sums for any other duties assigned to the Sponsor during his normal working day. The writer believes that this reasoning is fallacious; the by-product of it can only be resentment which can go a long way towards destroying the loyalty, enthusiasm and other qualities which were so greatly sought after in selecting the Sponsor.

Companies who understand that everyone likes to be rewarded or compensated for extra effort will find that the payment of a relatively small, additional sum of money either

SPONSOR PAYMENT

New employees must be employed a minimum of TWO WEEKS in the department for approval of Sponsor Payment.

Regular Employee (full or part–time) $1.00
Saturday & Evening 50
Seasonal 50
Rehire from another department 50
Rehire into same department . . . . No Payment
Transfer from other Selling Department . . . . No Payment
Contingent . . . . No Payment

THIS EMPLOYEE IS: (Please check one)

Regular full–time   ☐

Regular part–time   ☐

Saturday and Evening ☐

Seasonal   ☐

Rehire from another
    Department   ☐

SPONSOR: _____
                    Name   Date

DEPT. MGR. _____
                    Name   Date

SPONSOR: Please return this form to the Training Department.

weekly, monthly, or on a per capita basis will be greatly appreciated by the Sponsor. Another form of compensation is a gift certificate, which, in the case of department stores, can be spent right on the premises. It is also possible to compensate the Sponsor by giving him additional time off, either on a regular basis, or by permitting him to add it to his vacation. There are many ideas that can be used to show the Sponsor how much the company appreciates his efforts.

Recommended Reading (see Chapter 9)

Chapter Eight

Follow-up Training for All Employees

The title of this chapter is one of several names for the next phase of the overall training job to be considered. This phase is also referred to as "retraining" or "continuous training" because the training job is never done. There is a constant need for continuous follow-up training for all regular employees. This on-the-job aspect of training encompasses a wide range of activities from individual guidance in order to correct or improve individual employees, to company-wide assemblies which introduce new policies or methods. Thus, any activity used to improve an employee's job performance may be included in this phase of training.

Primarily, follow-up training is the responsibility of the Department Supervisor. There are some organizations which make both regular and sporadic efforts in this phase of the training job, but their number is few and far between. For example, one of the nation's most prominent department stores has a member of its Training Department designated as "the fashion floors" training representative. This individual is responsible for continually meeting with the various fashion apparel and accessory departments to keep them constantly aware of fashion trends and changes. She herself, of course, has to be able to secure this information by reading, research, and market visits. Other firms, from time to time, find it necessary to hold special classes primarily when they are introducing new systems, procedures or equipment; but the emphasis here is on the temporary nature of the training rather than on making this a permanent part of their follow-up training program. It is important to remember that the Department Supervisor can share his responsibility in this area of continuous training and delegate some of it, for example, to the Sponsor. This is particularly true when a new system or procedure or new equipment is being introduced. Such training requires the individual attention that only one person can give to another person. A Sponsor who has been trained to teach others by the J.I.T. method (to be discussed in Chapter Thirteen) is an ideal trainer for this phase of continuous training or retraining.

The following are but a few of the many things an alert Supervisor can do to help maintain his employees at their greatest level of efficiency in this continuous matter of follow-up training:

1. **Meetings**

    A company or a department meeting is one of the principal methods used in follow-up training. An actual problem arising out of recent activities, new merchandise, promulgation of new policy, re-emphasis on sales techniques, etc. are some of the ever-present items that can be discussed at such meetings. Of course, the meeting is planned and run by the Department Supervisor (see Chapter Ten).

2. **Manufacturer or Dealer Aids**

Many merchandise resources have a number of "dealer helps" that the energetic Manager may find extremely useful in follow-up training procedures. The larger companies frequently have excellent audiovisual aids available. Other manufacturers are happy to have members of their organization visit stores and help to train salespeople. Similarly, firms make it possible for professional demonstrators to train store personnel as well as to promote their own product. A tour through a plant or a visit to the market is also a very helpful training device.

3. **Outside Schooling**

There is an ever-increasing tendency on the part of resourceful Supervisors to take advantage of professional schooling opportunities whenever possible. The career-minded employee likewise regards this as one of the best types of follow-up training. In those cities where such evening college work is offered in merchandising or related business subjects, the firm would do well to encourage enrollment in such courses and to consider some form of tuition-subsidy, if necessary. It is also possible to arrange for special evening programs or adult education courses at the local high schools under the State's Distributive Education Program which is partly subsidized by the Federal Government. The local retail group or Chamber of Commerce can act as one of the sponsors for such a program. The use of outside experts to teach highly specialized groups of employees is also part of this trend. Shoe-fitting, corsetry, fashion, and new textiles are among the most common areas of special sales training frequently employing such professional teachers.

Recommended Reading (see Chapter 9)

Chapter Nine

Executive Training

A farsighted firm needs a plan for training its potential executives in order to insure continual growth and to secure a nucleus of career-minded employees. Of course, to attract the right people a company must develop a reputation for being a place that usually promotes its employees. The organization itself should recognize that there are distinct monetary advantages as well as morale factors that accrue from upgrading employees rather than hiring them away from other firms or competitors. Unfortunately, in too many instances, with all good intentions, people are promoted from within to their first executive or junior executive position with little or no training for this new responsibility. While it is laudatory that the company has seen fit to promote promising people, it is a fact of life that these neophytes do require assistance in learning the "whys and wherefores" of their new jobs. It is therefore incumbent upon the organization to see to it that the new Supervisor is adequately prepared.

EXECUTIVE RECRUITMENT

To paraphrase an old cliche: "Executives are not born, they are made." And before a potential executive can be "made," that is to say, trained and developed, he must be discovered or found. There are a number of resources from which the typical business organization may recruit people for development into executives:

1. **Colleges**

    This is probably a more important resource today as *the* place for recruiting executives than all other possible sources combined. As the overwhelming majority of those who will be using this book and reading this chapter can testify, there has been and continues to be a tremendous demand or drive on the part of American youth and their families for some sort of higher education. Industry has not been slow in taking note of this phenomena, and as a result, graduation from an institution of higher learning, or at least several years of college, has become the principal ticket of admission to a better or higher-paying position with any top-notch firm. It is little wonder, therefore, that the personnel representatives and recruiters from all phases of American industry make the college campus and/or its placement bureau their primary resource for discovering executive talent.

2. **Newspaper Advertisements**

    This is generally a method used to uncover potential junior executives who were either missed during a recruitment drive at the school level because they were away, or otherwise occupied, or because the recruiter was physically unable to handle the whole load. It is also a good secondary move to recruit people who might have taken a job and then discovered that the firm, the job, or the industry was not for them. Newspaper advertisements may also bring to light those people who have had a change of heart between the time they made their original selection and before the start of their employment. At any rate, the use of newspaper advertising to attract people to be trained as future executives must not be overlooked as a backup for other methods of executive recruitment.

3. **Executive Placement Agencies**

These were formerly known by the prosaic name of "employment agencies," and as such they still do a very helpful job in assisting those concerned with executive recruitment to supplement and complement their recruiting activities. Today these placement bureaus have taken on an aura of respectability as contrasted with the old line crass commercialism that was associated with the name "employment agency." Frequently the name of the bureau will include such terms as "executive search" or "personnel consultants." This form of executive recruitment is a strong secondary resource and should not be disregarded when it is necessary to complete the roster of a newly-forming executive training group. While these organizations formerly charged a fee to the applicant based upon a percentage of his starting salary, it is now customary for most large organizations using placement bureaus to pay this fee and even retain such organizations on an annual basis.

4. **Recommendations**

This is a minor factor in the recruiting of executive

personnel but one that still cannot be ignored. These referrals may come from various sources such as suppliers, friends or relatives of current employees or members of the firm; they can come from professionals who service the company such as bankers, lawyers, and accountants, and from educators who know of potential opportunities in the company.

5. Promotion from Within

This is a frequently overlooked potential source of executive talent because the average person who should be considered is *not*. This is due to the fact that he generally lacks the educational background that is now an almost mandatory prerequisite. This concern for the need of a college education, and the realization that people working for the firm may also have some potential, has even caused some large organizations to organize and conduct two distinct training programs, one on each level. While this "separate-but-equal" method is not widespread, it is indicative of the situation existing today. One of the ways that some firms have also met this problem is by encouraging, and in some cases, subsidizing the higher education of their employees in local evening colleges or courses in an effort to upgrade them for future consideration.

6. Piracy

This is usually a desperation measure when the sources of executive recruitment have seemingly been exhausted. Piracy is also used when there is little or no time for the firm to train one or more people for executive positions that need relatively immediate filling. At any rate, no matter what the cause or justification for this method of executive recruitment may be, it frequently has unpleasant connotations. It may cause a rash of piracy, particularly among a group of closely allied or competitive firms in an industry. It always causes higher wage costs and hard feelings. While the people being recruited may benefit financially from these actions, the possible repercussions frequently do not warrant this method. Piracy is usually accomplished by either executive search firms or by letting key suppliers or others outside the recruiting company do the "dirty work."

HOW SUPERVISORS ARE TRAINED

Once the recruitment process is over and the company has what it considers sufficient executive training material available from all sources, it is necessary to consider what form the training of these potential executives should take. There are a number of executive training methods now in current use, and these may be divided into two broad categories: (1) executive development which is carried on in groups; and (2) executive training that is done on an individual basis.

Group Training

This training for the job ahead is usually accomplished by means of an *Executive Training Squad*. The people who are selected for this group and the means of their recruitment have already been discussed earlier in this chapter. They are usually an elite group of people with previous merchandise training who have been carefully selected and screened by the Executive Placement Division of the Personnel Department; they are "predestined by fate" to become the future executives of the company. The Executive Training Squad is usually organized along the following lines:

1. **An organized classroom training program** built around a definite curriculum or course of study. The trainees are required to attend classes on a regularly-scheduled basis throughout a given period which may range from several months to a year or more. In a department store Executive Training Program, for example, regularly-scheduled classes are held in Merchandising, Buying, Sales Promotion, and Executive Leadership. The courses are taught by members of the Training Department and are supplemented by guest lectures by top executives of each of the store's divisions who are specialists in a particular field. The trainees are tested regularly and given assignments and projects relating to their work. Such a course is designed as a crash-program in order to get the newcomer to the field on to the first rung of the executive ladder as soon as possible.

2. **A job rotation program** is usually coupled with the above-mentioned classroom training. By this method, the executive trainee is moved on a regularly scheduled basis from one major area or division or department to another for a definitely-designated period which may last from several days to several weeks. In this way, the trainee not only gains an insight into the working of the entire company as well as valuable experience, but he is also exposed to the major facets of the firm's operation and its executives. Thus, on the days when the trainee is not in class, he may be working.

This type of training was originated primarily for the liberal arts graduate who had not been business-oriented until graduation time. In recent years, the rapid growth and tremendous development of junior or community college programs in business, marketing and merchandising, have caused many organizations to shorten or modify such programs for this new type of trainee.

In the training of a group of junior executives, whether it is in the formal classroom-structured program previously discussed, or in a less formal instruction group, there are a number of training techniques that can be profitably employed.

- **a.** *Conferences* bring together small groups of trainees to consider problems in a joint effort to solve them. (See Chapter Eleven.)

- **b.** *Meetings* bring all the trainees together in a lecture-like set-up to learn from the meeting leader. (See Chapter Ten.)

- **c.** *Case Studies* use actual or structured cases which have a direct relationship to the work being studied by the executive trainees. By analyzing the cases, they will not only gain an insight into the common problems faced by Supervisors, but they will learn to become analytical.

- **d.** *Role-Playing* is the enactment of a real work situation and involves not only the role players but those watching, as well, since they identify with the player. (See Chapter Twelve.)

- **e.** *Committees* get the trainees to learn to work in small groups in a survey, a fact-gathering or problem-solving project.

- **f.** *Brain-Storming* brings the trainees together in a group where they are given a question of common interest. The members of the group are asked to put forth any ideas, no matter how wild or impractical, which they may see at the moment. These suggestions are recorded or put on a blackboard. Members may "piggy-back" on the ideas of others, but they may never give a negative answer or say "no" or object to any ideas given; only positive suggestions are accepted. After the group has exhausted its ideas on the subject, the most impractical ones are eliminated and the rest may be used for future work.

Individual Training

There are some training authorities who feel that executive training done on a one-to-one relationship is superior to the group training previously discussed. They argue that this method lends itself to a closer relationship between the executive doing the training and the beginner. They say that learning is more rapid and effective when there is informality and an absence of rigidity that arises from scheduling. It should be pointed out, however, that the entire success of the whole individual training program rests on one factor — the person designated to do the training. If he is a good instructor, willing and able to communicate, enthusiastic, knowledgeable, patient, and tactful, then the executive trainee will be well-served; if not, the training will not only be doomed to failure from the start, but it will probably cost the company the loss of the trainee and the time, money, and effort the training involved.

There are a number of training techniques that can be used in the individual training method.

1. **Job Rotation** has been discussed in the section on Group Training. The student will recall that the executive trainee is routed through a number of different departments and placed in a variety of different positions. This is done, not only to teach him the workings of various jobs and acquaint him with a

broad spectrum of the organization, but also allows him to be observed in action on the job as he rotates from area to area of the company. The trainee is also exposed to the many aspects of the supervisory job as it exists in each department.

2. **On-The-Job-Training (O.J.T.)** is in direct contrast to *Job Rotation* as an individual training method. The trainee is usually confined to one department or unit of the company and works under one Supervisor during his entire training period. It can be likened to the old apprenticeship method where the trainee sat at the foot of the master and learned his superior's job. This is the most commonly used of all the individual executive training methods.

3. **The Executive Flying Squad** is primarily a department store training technique used by stores that do not wish to make a large investment in a formal group Executive Training Squad. The regular Flying Squad is normally made up of contingents who are assigned on a daily or even hourly basis to places in the store where they are needed most. The Executive Flying Squad operates in exactly the same fashion. However, instead of being mere rank-and-file employees without a real assignment, the executive trainees on this squad are carefully-selected, college-trained, junior executive material working on a junior executive wage scale. While some of the nation's finest retail establishments use this form of individual executive training, its faults are so apparent that the writer cannot see any justification for its existence. What the trainee can really learn in such a haphazard rotation manner is so infinitesimal, and the constant shifting from one demeaning job to another is so derogatory, that the less said about the *Executive Flying Squad,* the better.

4. **"In-Basket" Techniques** is a decision-making training device which derives its name from the material an executive might normally find in his "in" basket on his desk. This tray is loaded with memoranda, reports, notes, requests, forms, telephone messages, letters, circulars, etc. During this training period which may be one hour, for example, he goes through the "in" basket and answers or takes care of as many items as possible. At the end of the hour, his "out" basket is examined. The trainee then discusses his decisions on the items handled as well as those he selected for action, and why.

5. **Outside Schooling and Programs** as the name implies, is a phase of individual training which takes place outside the company. Outside programs are primarily provided by professional management or trade associations which conduct seminars and workshops. The other aspect of outside training is provided by technical institutes, schools, colleges and university centers. Some firms encourage and frequently subsidize the enrollment of executive trainees in courses, as well as for degrees. These schools also conduct special seminars for industry in various areas.

6. **Combination of the Above.** It should be pointed out that the five above-mentioned individual executive training techniques are not necessarily confined to use one-at-a-time within an organization. It is not unusual for a firm to use one or more of these in combinations that are best suited to the company and its needs.

Recommended Reading

Beckman: How To Train Supervisors — pp. 212-225

Craig and Bittel: Training & Development Handbook — Chapters 1, 2, 18, 19, 23

Section IV

Training Techniques

Chapter Ten

Conducting a Department Meeting

One of the normal duties of the Supervisor is to hold meetings with members of his staff on a regular and/or an informal basis. Many firms require Department Heads to hold regularly-scheduled (e.g., weekly) meetings with their subordinates. Some of these companies even expect the Manager to send a summary of the proceedings to top management. In addition, there will be frequent occasions when the Supervisor will find it necessary to meet informally with his staff or perhaps with some key people. The primary purpose of this meeting, no matter how formal or informal it is, is usually to *give* information to the group, although sometimes meetings might be called to *get* information from them.

As indicated in Chapter Eight, the meeting is the primary tool in follow-up or continuous training. By means of the department meeting the Supervisor can keep his staff current on all pertinent matters; he can introduce new methods, systems, and procedures, and generate team spirit to encourage better production (sales).

Before we undertake to determine how to hold good department meetings, it is essential that we have a firm understanding of what a meeting is and how it is conducted. A meeting is an assembly of employees who are gathered together by their Supervisor in order to cover a definite amount of information as quickly as possible. The physical set-up is like that of a classroom, because the chairs all face one focal point — the place where the Supervisor or meeting leader stands. The number of people who can attend a meeting is only limited by the space available.

The leader is the key person in the meeting. He is the source of information which he delivers by means of the lecture method. Group participation either in the form of questions from the floor or by discussion among individuals in the group is helpful, but the fact remains that it is the leader's responsibility to cover the topics adequately.

Planning is the essence of holding a good meeting. When one employee says to another, "Well, it's our department meeting again, today," and the reply comes back loud and clear, "Ugh," the reason is usually apparent: boring, unorganized, unplanned meetings that do nothing to *interest* the staff.

To help assure the success of this vital form of training and communication, the Supervisor should consider the following principles in conducting his staff or department meetings.

Know What You Want To Do!

The Supervisor must have a definite purpose for conducting the meeting. If this first step in planning the meeting is not carried out thoughtfully and carefully, the meeting is doomed to failure before it begins. It is also a general principle not to try to cover too much at one time. One topic is usually sufficient and advisable. Most organizations do not have time for long meetings during the working day; lengthy meetings soon pall on those attending.

Know Your Stuff!

Confidence in the leader goes out the window when it becomes apparent that he has only a little or a superficial knowledge of his subject. This requires, at times, reading or research for the Manager in preparation for his talk. At a recent department meeting one salesperson whispered to another, "He (the Manager) doesn't know what he's talking about; the facts really are . . . " A question from the floor can catch the Supervisor unprepared, and the loss of face that can follow may prove irreparable.

Motivate Your Listeners!

It is not enough that the leader have a purpose that he wants his meeting to accomplish. It is equally important that those who attend should understand how *they* will benefit as a result of the proceedings. "What's in it for me" is an old but true cliche. Wherever possible the Supervisor should tactfully make the beneficial aspect of the employees' attendance open and apparent.

Be Different and Versatile!

"Here comes the same old baloney"; or "It's the same stuff every week." If these comments are heard around the meeting room, then it's time for a change. While the lecture method dominates the average meeting, it can be enlivened with a variety of material. Among the techniques the

Supervisor can use to vary his meetings are:

1. **Films** — dealing with topics of current interest are available from manufacturers, rental firms, schools, etc.

2. **Charts** — made by the leader or the Display Department help to add clarity and interest to the talk.

3. **A Blackboard** — makes it possible to jot down key points and helps to focus the group's attention.

4. **Guest Speakers** — from merchandise resources, the company's own executive staff, manufacturer's demonstrators, etc.

5. **Role-Playing** — using department personnel to act out ideas. (See Chapter Twelve.)

6. **Demonstrations** — such as informal fashion shows help to demonstrate the talk; live merchandise or materials always make a more permanent impression than a discussion of them.

7. **Group Discussion** — a technique that always encourages more communication than the less free-wheeling lecture approach.

All seven items above require some "props" to be effective. These items must be secured or prepared in advance of the meeting. Nothing can be more disconcerting than the poorly prepared leader who realizes in the midst of the meeting that he needs a "prop" to make his point. In addition to things that may help to illustrate the lecture, there are, of course, standard supplies needed for many meetings such as:

1. **Chairs** — an adequate number arranged so that all attention is directed to the leader.

2. **Ash Trays** — if smoking is permitted on the meeting premises.

3. **Paper and Pencil** — if note-taking is necessary or desirable.

4. **Printed Materials** — forms, manufacturer's brochures, manuals, mimeos, etc.

5. **Speaker's Stand** — lectern, podium or table for the meeting leader and his material.

6. **Amplification System (microphone and speakers)** — if a large space is needed or provided.

It is quite important as part of this physical aspect of planning for the meeting that the room be adequately lighted and well ventilated. It should also be free from distracting noises or activity.

Know What You Want To Say!

The heart of the meeting, of course, is "the lecture" delivered by the Supervisor or meeting leader. The following are some important considerations in the planning and delivery of the information.

1. Write out the key points — do not write a speech — make some notes on a card or paper.

2. Do not read your talk — nothing could be more boring and less confidence-building. Refer to notes, but know your topic well enough to speak easily.

3. Don't ramble on — be brief and to the point.

4. Don't try to cover too much — stick to one important topic or phase thereof.

5. Be enthusiastic about your topic — the Supervisor's enthusiasm must infect the group; his lack of enthusiasm can smother the group's hopes and ambitions.

6. Plan the opening very carefully — it is important to hold the group's attention from the start. There are three important types of openings:

    a. **The ancedotal approach** — tell a story, joke or anecdote which is related to or fits in with the topic to be discussed.

    b. **The shocking or provocative statement** — "Do you know that according to reliable statistics, one person out of ten could lose an eye out of carelessness?" the leader of a meeting on safety might begin. The shocking statement is one that will jolt the audience into thinking along the lines the leader desires.

    c. **The salutation method** — is the ordinary method of greeting the group politely with a salutation such as: "Hello everyone, glad you could all get here."

7. Get the group into the act! Encourage and plan for the maximum amount of group participation that the time and topic will allow. Employees and students react in the same way to the lecture method — they soon get fed up; they want variety;

they want to get into the act. The alert Supervisor can capitalize on this natural reaction to help insure a more fruitful meeting.

Begin and Close On Time!

Promptness is not only a virtue, it is also usually a business necessity. The department or staff meeting is normally restricted to a limited time slot and the leader must make the most of it. Careful planning for the meeting must also include closing on time. It is very annoying to the group to hear the leader say, "I'm sorry, that's all the time we have today. We'll try to finish this up next time." This indicates poor planning and poor execution. If the Supervisor wishes to end properly, he can ask one of the group to signal him well ahead of time so that he can bring the proceedings to a normal close.

The close of the meeting should always include a brief summation by the leader in which he reaffirms the principles, policies, etc. covered in the meeting.

Be Sure To Follow Up!

It is not enough to lecture, harangue, or exhort the group. An integral part of the meeting is what happens afterwards. Did the listeners learn anything? Are they doing as instructed? These questions can only be answered by a follow-up — either through direct observation by the Supervisor or by the checking of records. The real success of meetings comes from a persistent, calculated follow-up by the Supervisor. Only in this way can the Supervisor know that what he has taught has taken hold.

Meetings are an important method of reaching employees for communication and training purposes. To be successful, they must be well planned; if they are well planned they will be interesting.

Recommended Reading

A.M.A.: Leadership on the Job — pp. 68-73

Craig and Bittel: Training & Development Handbook — Chapter 8

Halsey, George: Supervising Employees — Chapter 11

Halsey, George: Training Employees — Chapter 9

Chapter Eleven

The Conference Method

Along with its normal function of solving problems, the conference, as indicated in Chapter Nine, is an important method of training executives. The conference is a form of meeting in which the participants endeavor to learn from one another. In this method of executive training, the conferees pool their knowledge and experience to solve their own, as well as the group's, problems. It can be inferred that those attending a conference are all more or less on the same level and that all have relatively similar experience; at least they must all have the capacity to analyze the problem under discussion.

There is a frequent tendency to confuse the conference with the meeting because, as indicated previously, the conference is one of several types of meetings. There is no real basis for this confusion because:

1. In a meeting the participants learn from the leader; in a conference, they learn from each other.

2. In a meeting there is no limit to the size of the group; the conference must be limited in size in order for the participation to be active and involved — the usual size is 3 to 20, with 12 to 15 being the best average.

3. In the meeting, the leader dominates the proceedings; in the conference, the leader must never dominate — he *guides* the group's thinking and discussion.

4. In the meeting, attention is focused on the leader by virtue of the physical set-up of the room — like a classroom; in a conference the group preferably uses a round or oval table set-up (or the chairs are put in a circle if no such table is available).

These are but a few of the differences that set the conference and meeting apart and they should not require any further differentiation.

It has been said by leading authorities in the field of executive training that the success or failure of the conference as a method of training depends a great deal upon the leadership of the group. Accordingly, we would do well to examine those qualities of conference leadership that make for the ideal leader, in order to select and develop trainees or executives along those lines.

1. The good conference leader should be expert in stimulating others to discuss the subject on hand; he need not have expertise in that subject himself, but he should know how to handle people coolly and impartially.

2. He must know how to prevent an individual from monopolizing the group's time, so that all the others can contribute.

3. He is never a teacher or lecturer; he never tells anyone anything — neither what to say nor what to think nor what to do. He does not talk too much because he knows that if he does, the members of the group will talk less or not at all.

4. He must be able to get the group to assemble, select and evaluate all of the facts in order to provoke a group discussion.

5. He should be an analytically clear thinker in order to help guide the group in its analysis of the problem.

6. He must be impersonal, patient, unbiased, tactful, enthusiastic, poised and self-restrained. If he is not this paragon of virtue, it will be difficult for him to truly exercise his role of leader, judge, conciliator and interpreter.

If a conference is only as good as its leadership, then it must follow that the leader is only as good as his preparations for leading the conference. To be adequately prepared to lead a conference, the leader's preparation should involve the following:

1. He should be thoroughly familiar and up-to-date with the subject matter to be discussed. This involves keeping up his reading of all available current periodicals and books.

2. He should prepare a plan or agenda for the conference and become thoroughly familiar with this plan.

3. He should secure adequate conference room facilities. The conference room should be large, adequately lit and well ventilated.

4. He should secure all necessary supplies such as pads, pencils, ash-trays, blackboard (if to be used), name/place cards, etc. The room should preferably be furnished with a round or oval table; if a table is not available, the chairs should be arranged in a circle.

5. He should arrange to have the participants notified (preferably in writing) that their attendance is required and ask that they prepare, or at least think about, the topic or problem before the conference.

CONFERENCE PROCEDURE

After carefully planning for the conference, the day and hour for it arrives and the participants assemble in the conference room. The following can be considered a typical conference procedure, although it should be made clear that there is a great deal of room for variety and improvisation.

The Opening

The conference must get off to a good start in order to help insure its successful conclusion. The following factors should be considered for a good opening:

1. The leader should open the conference and put the conferees at ease by greeting them in a manner similar to that discussed in Chapter Ten.

2. The conference should be opened with introductions all around the table if any or all of the conferees are strangers to one another.

3. The purpose of the conference and the topic to be discussed should be announced by the leader.

4. An expression of hope by the leader that there will be full participation, so that the free exchange of ideas will permit the participants to learn from one another and to help solve the problems at hand.

Developing Group Discussion and Participation

The most important part of the conference method, after the opening has been accomplished, is to have the group led smoothly into its main purpose: to develop a going discussion with full participation by all the conferees. The leader must make sure that everyone takes an active part in the discussion; he should then begin to take a back seat, fading into the background. There are a number of devices or techniques that can be used to obtain this goal.

1. The leader may throw out a question in order to get individual opinions. When someone answers, the leader can throw out another question or make a statement based on that answer or opinion. Then he can ask the others' opinion of *his* reply, etc.

2. He must stimulate and encourage questions from the group, to be answered by others in the group.

3. The leader must not only keep the discussion moving, but he must keep it on the subject.

4. The leader should encourage friendly differences of opinion.

5. The use of the blackboard to record ideas and contributions is considered a good technique. It

gives recognition to the contributor and keeps the ideas before the group.

Despite all of his good intentions and efforts, the leader may find that one or more of these commonly-occurring problems:

1. **The problem of the eager beaver** — this is an intelligent, alert, and aggressive group member who has one ambition in the conference — to dominate it by answering as many of the questions as possible, or by giving an opinion on every answer.

    Recommended Solutions:

    a. Give him the recognition he wants by saying: "Mr. Brown, you know how we value your contributions BUT, I'm sure you can see the need of hearing from some of the others who have not spoken yet."

    b. Fail to recognize him as often as you can; don't look in his direction!

2. **The problem of the shy person** is an anomaly if there ever was one. This presents the situation of an executive (or executive trainee) who is by definition a leader. There is seemingly no place in such a person's makeup for timidity, and yet the shyness is evidenced by a complete lack of participation in the conference. Since it is the leader's duty to elicit full participation, this paradox must be resolved.

    Recommended Solution:

    The shy person's reticence is probably due to a

feeling of insecurity with members of his group; he is probably "a lion" in his own department or environment. To bring him into the mainstream of discussion, the leader should throw him an easy question, one that he can handle easily and well. The leader should commend him, make a fuss over the answer, and refer to it as "his" answer or contribution from time to time.

3. **The problem of the argumentative person** is analagous to the problem of the nasty drunk. He wants to quibble over every other word or triviality. In other words: he argues just for the sake of arguing.

   Recommended Solutions:

   a. Leader should keep cool and not get personally involved.

   b. Call for a vote by the group to settle that point.

   c. Ask him questions that could draw him out and perhaps settle him down or make him look foolish enough in front of the others, so that he will shut up in shame.

4. **The problem of the tangential person** is not as serious a problem as the three previously enumerated ones. It is quite natural to expect that the leader will have to step in from time to time and bring the discussion "back on the beam" when so many articulate people are involved. Some people find it easy to go off on a tangent and the leader's job is to correct the situation.

Recommended Solutions:

    a.   Tactfully ask the person at fault how this point (the tangential one) can contribute to the topic at hand. If it has some relationship, he will make his point; otherwise he will drop the subject in a hurry.

    b.   Tactfully interrupt the person who has gone off on a tangent and say: "That sounds like an interesting topic, but it ought to have a conference of its own some day. May we now, however, return to the problem assigned?"

Keeping the Conference Moving Evenly

With the conference opened, discussion moving freely, and participation at a good level, the conference leader's task is to keep the conference moving along in accordance with the agenda he has prepared. The conference leader also has the job of keeping his fingers on the conference's pulse. When the rate at which the conference moves is *slow*, the members tend to devote too much time to minutiae — "nit picking." This can only serve to delay the outcome of the conference. Where the tempo is *fast*, the talk becomes too succinct or laconic to be of any real value as discussion. Thus, the leader needs to learn to accelerate or slow down the pace of the conference by his manner of speech and/or by his body movements.

    1.   **Manner of Speech** — when the leader is using a relaxed, casual, conversational tone of voice, it encourages the conferees to proceed at a free and easy pace. If he uses a sharp precise, incisive speech pattern, it makes the conferees and the conference move forward more rapidly.

2. **Body Movements** — when the conference leader is seated, he seems to be inviting continued discussion. But when he arises from his seat, for example, to go to the blackboard to write down a key point or idea, or when he is at the board summarizing, all talking stops and the pace is speeded.

Another aspect of this phase of the conference procedure is the leader's obligation to bring out into the open and encourage in a friendly way, as many differences of opinion as may exist among the conferees. However, it should be clearly understood that the leader must remain impartial throughout the conference proceedings and he must neither take sides nor try to settle these differences himself. Whenever a dispute arises in the conference and it has been adequately discussed, the leader calls for a vote and the group consensus settles the disagreement.

Summarizing Frequently

As the conference is kept moving along on an even keel by the conference leader, it is considered good form by the leading authorities in this field for him to summarize what the group has accomplished after each important point or item has been agreed on. To settle each major item on the agenda as it is reached by the group, the leader says something like: "O.K., as I understand it, we are agreed that . . ." If anyone raises an objection at this point, the leader then puts the question to a vote and lets majority rule settle it. The leader then records the point on the blackboard or, if none is being used, the group recorder is directed to make note of the agreed-upon fact. As each point of agreement is reached, the leader should summarize the progress to date — restating and re-emphasizing what has been discussed and agreed upon.

Final Summarizing and Concluding The Conference

The conference leader, like the meeting leader (see Chapter Ten), has to watch the time. He must be sure that sufficient time is allotted for a summarization of the highlights of the conference. The summary need not be lengthy, but with the help of his conferees, the leader should leave them with a clear impression of the conclusions and solutions that they arrived at after evaluating ideas, opinions, suggestions and experiences.

The leader should then express his thanks and perhaps the gratitude of the management for their presence and their assistance.

Follow-Up

The followup procedure takes place a short time after the conference. The leader should polish up the summarization referred to previously. A copy of the agreed-upon findings should be sent to all the participants to make a more lasting impression on them. It is also important for a report to be filed with the leader's superiors and any other management division that might be involved or interested.

To conclude this chapter, it would be well to evaluate the value Conference Leadership as a form of training Supervisors and other executives by acting as conference leaders and participants.

1. It helps to develop the group's tolerance of one another and the ability to understand the ideas, opinions, and suggestions of others.

2. It helps to develop the leader's skill in getting others to contribute such ideas, suggestions and opinions in the

most creative ways possible.

3. It helps to make the leader become a better conference participant now that he knows what is expected of a conferee from the leader's point of view.

4. It helps to develop both the leader's and the participants' ability to express their ideas in public and to learn how these ideas are received by others. This ability to express oneself clearly is an important asset in supervision and leadership.

5. It helps to improve the leader's ability to train people because conference leadership is closely allied to the training skills needed by all Supervisors. It is good training to lead his own staff meetings, an important function in supervision.

Recommended Reading

A.M.A.: A Guide to Successful Conference Leadership

Beach: Personnel – The Management of People at Work – Chapter 18

Craig and Bittel: Training and Development Handbook – Chapter 9

Dooher and Marquis: Effective Communication On The Job – Chapter 8

Halsey: Training Employees – Chapter 4

Planty and Freeston: Developing Management Ability – Chapter 8

Section V

Supervisory Principles and Techniques

Chapter Twelve

Role-Playing

Role-playing is a training technique utilizing two or more people who act out a given part in a simulated real-life situation. It is the *dramatization* of a commonly occurring situation or problem. Most modern training programs today include role-playing on all the levels of training: initial, follow-up, and executive.

Training authorities have made much of the values in role-playing that are seemingly absent from other forms of learning such as the lecture method. Most learning is "acquired" by reading or listening and then writing; it is *non-participating.* Role-playing is learning by doing, by imitating, by observing, by experimenting, by practicing; these are followed by analyzing and forming concepts. Role-playing, thus, is *participatory*.

HISTORY AND BACKGROUND

Role-playing has an interesting history and background. The "invention" of role-playing is generally credited to Dr. J. L. Moreno, a Viennese psychiatrist who later emigrated to this country. "Pyschodrama" or "Sociodrama" was originated by Dr. Moreno who employed role-playing primarily in group psychotherapy, which he used to make psychiatric treatment available at low rates to more people. The Moreno Institute is located in New York City, and for a small fee, people who feel they are in need of treatment for emotional or behavioral problems may attend and participate. As this pioneer work progressed, many variations of the technique emerged. Through reports in newspapers and magazines it came to the attention of industrial psychologists and training experts who quickly realized its potential as a group training device. It is now widely used in many forms, and recently it received great impetus by its use in business games, simulations and problem-solving projects, particularly in the training of executives.

FORMS OF ROLE-PLAYING

It should be emphasized at the outset that there are literally hundreds of variations of the role-playing technique and there are very few clear dividing lines among them. We can use two *broad* classifications in approaching this area of training: (1) Structured (pre-planned) role-playing; and (2) Spontaneous (unplanned) role-playing.

1. **Structured role-playing** refers to the amount of *instruction* or preparation given by the trainer or leader (role-playing director) to those playing the roles. He outlines the problem to them, but does not tell the players what or how to say or do. Thus, the role-playing is being "structured" to a pre-planned problem or

situation. We will be concerned for the balance of this chapter with the "structured" approach to role-playing because we are primarily interested in role-playing as a training technique in specific instances.

2. **Spontaneous role-playing** involves very little, if any, direction to the players by the leader or director. The group selects a meaningful problem and, without guidance, proceeds to respond freely to forces, drives, behavior patterns, etc., at the same time interpreting and analyzing their findings.

USES OF ROLE-PLAYING IN SUPERVISION

Before we proceed to break down the role-playing technique in an effort to teach the Supervisor or executive trainee how to use it, we would do well to review briefly the applications of role-playing to actual training situations. It has been repeatedly said that this training technique has almost unlimited uses in training both individuals and groups in any area where there is a need for increasing effectiveness in interpersonal relations — where people have to deal with others. A small, incomplete list of training situations involving the interaction of two or more people, where skills, policies, or change of behavior are desired, includes:

1. **Interviewing** — employment, corrective, or grievances.

2. **Sponsor Training** — teaching Sponsors how and what to teach.

3. **Appraisal Reviews** — going over an employee's merit rating form.

4. **Handling the Public** — refunds, adjustments, exchanges etc.

5. **Selling Techniques** — all phases of selling.

6. **Training Leaders** — conferences, business games simulations, and case studies.

THE "MECHANICS" OF ROLE-PLAYING

As a reminder to the reader, we must recall that role-playing has many applications, variations and differences in methodology and interpretation. This author feels, however, that the following method is a sound, middle-of-the-road technique that will serve the average Supervisor well. These factors in exploring the "mechanics" of role-playing will be discussed:

A. The physical setting or place.

B. The group.

C. The leader or role-playing director.

D. The players.

E. The "structure," or roles or case to be acted out.

F. The role-playing procedure.

A. The Place

Role-playing does not require any *special* type of physical set-up. It can be done in a conference room, a classroom, or a large office. There are several important factors:

1. There should be provisions for privacy — the room should be free from interruptions of all kinds.

2. There should be flexible seating — movable chairs are necessary in order to arrange them in a semicircle. In the front of the room, in the middle of the semicircle, a table or desk and chairs for the role players should be provided.

3. All materials needed for the role-playing should be at hand. For example, in a sales training situation, merchandise, salesbooks, etc., should be available.

4. Lighting arrangements can be a plus factor since role-playing is a dramatization. The audience should sit in darkness or in dim lights, the players in good, strong lighting.

B. The Group

A real knowledge of the group engaged in a role-playing situation is very helpful to the leader who can then tailor the role-playing to fit the group's needs. The goal of role-playing is to teach the group something or to change an attitude or behavior pattern by means of group identification with the players. It is therefore logical to expect that knowing your audience will be valuable.

C. The Leader

The person directing the role-playing is generally called the leader. The person will, of course, vary, depending on who is doing the training. The department head frequently runs the show; at other times it might be a training department representative, etc. In our description of the "structure" the reader will soon see how large and important a part the leader plays in this training technique.

D. The Players

While the players who actually engage in the role-playing benefit the most from this form of training, carefully selected players, quite representative of either the roles or the group or both, can cause the entire group to identify with them, thus attaining the primary purpose of the session. It is especially interesting if one or more of the players is a true-life characterization of the role. Some role-playing leaders like to rely on the use of spontaneous volunteers from the audience just before the role-playing is scheduled to begin. This generally precludes the possibility of the leader being able to make as careful a selection as possible. Care and deliberation in the "casting" of the players well before the session is therefore a good idea.

E. The "Structure"

The structured role playing method may be likened to a case study, except that in role-playing the material is presented verbally, while the case study data is written. The department Supervisor or Training Director (or whoever is using role-playing as a training technique) must select a problem area that the trainees are in or may face in the future. The leader must pinpoint such things as the background of the problem, and determine what roles the players are to play (tell them *who* they are). During the preparation of the "structure," the leader must continually keep his goal for the session in mind. He must be guided by what he hopes the role-playing will accomplish.

F. The Procedure

With all the preparation completed, the actual role-playing may now begin. But the mere dramatization of a real-life work situation is only a hopeful exercise in verbal fireworks. The exchange of conversation between two or more people can be interesting, but it is incomplete unless what occurs "on stage" is thoroughly discussed, analyzed, and understood by the entire training group. Thus the role-playing procedure may be broken down as follows:

1. Assigning roles to players.

2. The enactment.

3. Bringing the enactment to a close.

4. Evaluation.

   a. Self-evaluation by the players.

   b. Cross-evaluation by the players.

   c. Evaluation by the group.

   d. Evaluation by the leader.

5. Summary and conclusion.

1. Assigning roles to players

Using the pre-planned "structure" or roles determined in his preparation, the leader tells each player *who* he is and what his particular background is in the case. It should be noted that while each player's role is given to him in full sight and sound of the group, the other players or player are not present and must be out of hearing range. In other words, each player only has a vague idea of the role of the other. The players are urged to *immerse* themselves in their roles; they must try to portray their assigned role and character as they envision it; or at least to simulate the role to the best of their ability. The audience should be advised to take notes and should be cautioned to remain absolutely quiet throughout the enactment. They must be strictly warned about laughing or snickering at the players, who frequently have a hard enough time as it is. In concluding this first step of the role-playing procedure, the leader would do well to be sure that all parties thoroughly understand the "structure" and the individual roles. This means that the leader should encourage questions from all concerned in order to clarify the entire situation.

2. **The enactment**

It is now time for the players to be brought face to face and put into positions; for example, the Supervisor seated behind the desk and the employee about to enter his office, or perhaps seated in the interviewee's chair. Hopefully, the players, having determined that they wish to see a fruitful and successful role-playing session, will completely immerse themselves in their respective roles and enact their parts as they really see them. The leader, who has retired to the sidelines after assigning the roles, must follow these proceedings very closely, taking notes if possible.

3. **Bringing the enactment to a close**

   The leader's next important function in the role-playing procedure is to know *when* to bring the enactment to a close. Several factors will dictate when this procedure should take place:

   a. If the players come to a natural close within the time available, the leader's job will have been done for him by the players. This may be called the *natural* close and it is much to be desired in role-playing.

   b. There are several factors which may force the leader to bring the enactment to a close such as: time running out; the conversation beginning to drag and the players having apparently exhausted their roles; or the players beginning to repeat themselves as if they were going around in circles, which is also indicative that a closing is in order. The leader, therefore, brings the enactment to an *artificial* close by saying: "I think we have heard enough to give us a good idea..."

4. **Evaluation**

   a. *Self-evaluation by the players* — When the enactment has been brought to a close, the first order of business during the evaluation period is to have each player evaluate his own performance. The leader should encourage this evaluation, if necessary, by asking each player to answer such questions as:

   "Now that the dramatization is over, if you

had it to do all over again, would you act the same way as you just did?"

"Do you really picture yourself in real life doing just what you did?"

"Do you think you were too lenient (or too strict)?" "What would you change if you had a second chance?" ... etc., etc.

Each player makes this type of evaluation under the guidance of the leader.

b. *Cross-evaluation* — The leader then requires the players to evaluate each other. If necessary, the leader should "feed" questions such as:

"Did you find the Supervisor fair in his treatment of you?"

"Do you think you would respect him more if he were stricter with you?"

"If you were in his place — reversing roles — what would you have done?" ...etc., etc.

Again, this second evaluation period is done under the supervision of the role-playing session leader.

c. *Evaluation by the group* — For all intents and purposes, this is probably the *most* important part of the entire role-playing procedure. If the role-playing session is to be considered at all successful, all or most of the training group must *identify* with the actions of either or both of the players. And the only way that the leader will have any knowledge of whether this has occurred is by the response he gets at this point in the procedure. The leader will usually find the members of the group eager and willing to take sides, and in any other way to evaluate what they have seen and heard. Because there will be a great many volunteers at this point it is not usually necessary for the leader to call on individual members of the group. He should, nevertheless, be prepared to call on people directly and ask them questions similar to the ones mentioned in the self- and cross-evaluation proceedings described above.

This portion of the evaluation period may proceed for as long as the time allotted allows.

d. *Evaluation by the leader* — The leader's critique brings the evaluation period to a close. It is his privilege to evaluate the players as well as the audience's criticism. He should particularly point out to the group how and when it identified with the players or the situation.

The leader may also indicate at this point how he felt the enactment should have proceeded or what he hoped the players would have done. In other words, he describes what he would have done if he were one, or even both, of the players.

5. **Summary**

> The remaining moments of the role-playing session are taken up by the leader's summation and his attempts to arrive at some definite conclusions as a result of both the enactment and the evaluation. The group should not be dismissed until it has been made aware of the lesson that the role-playing situation has tried to teach.

In bringing this chapter to a close, the writer would like to recommend the use of closed-circuit television with instant replay, if it is available, as an audiovisual aid. He has successfully used this media in his own classes at the Fashion Institute of Technology with very interesting results, particularly during the evaluation period. It is a natural thing for the players to forget something they did or said, and in the course of the evaluation, the leader may ask the audiovisualist to replay that portion of the video-tape which depicts the real portrayal. This enrichment serves to make role-playing one of the best training techniques in vogue today.

Recommended Reading

Craig and Bittel: Training & Development Handbook — Chapter 11

Flippo: Principles of Personnel Management — pp. 225-226

Strauss and Sayles: Personnel: The Human Problems of Management — pp. 565-566

Chapter Thirteen

J.I.T. – Job Instructor Training

The initials J.I.T. stand for Job Instructor Training. It is a training technique that is used extensively in many aspects of our nation's economy — industry, retailing, finance, commerce, institutions and government. By the J.I.T. technique all types of business enterprises are training job instructors to teach the job *once*, and to teach it correctly. In other words, J.I.T. is a method of teaching those whose job it is to teach others *how* to teach properly.

WHO NEEDS TO USE J.I.T.?

Anyone involved with breaking in people on a job will find J.I.T. invaluable because this method builds all the key points of the position right into the training process and then provides for follow-up. It is a step-by-step process that assumes that the training the worker receives must include all of the elements he will need to start out strongly. This means, therefore, that Supervisors need to be proficient in the techniques of J.I.T. if they, themselves, are responsible for training their subordinates. Or, if they delegate all or part of their training duties to some competent person (such as an Assistant Supervisor, a senior employee, or a "Sponsor"), the Supervisor must first teach this person how to use the J.I.T. method of teaching. Thus, this newly-trained person will be in a position to teach the job to future newcomers to the department.

HISTORY AND DEVELOPMENT OF J.I.T.

The J.I.T. method came into being as a result of the production crisis brought on by World War II in 1941-42. Millions of workers came or were forced into war production jobs with absolutely no previous experience or training. And to make things worse, the people who had the responsibility for supervising this great mass of untrained workers were themselves poorly trained. In general, they had never done the jobs they were supposed to teach. The Training-Within-Industry (T.W.I.) division of the United States War Production Board was quickly established and the leading training directors of the country were given the problem of formulating a training program that could make trainers out of Supervisors. Overnight the J.I.T. program became the answer that trained over 13 million new workers within an amazingly short period of time. This relatively simple training technique (J.I.T.) was taught to thousands of Supervisors who in turn used it to teach these millions of workers thousands of different jobs and skills. The result was a flood of goods that not only equipped the American armed forces of 11 million, but all of our allies as well.

J.I.T. TODAY

After the war was over, industry saw the continued value of J.I.T. and it is still widely used today. The United States Department of Labor has estimated that in the decade of the sixties, over 26 million people joined the labor force in all branches of employment. Very few of them had any experience for their new jobs. Training them required the manager to know a specific and tested method of teaching a job to an employee. Where the J.I.T. method was correctly used it was unsurpassed in this regard. When employed properly, J.I.T. cannot fail. A simple test is available to the supervisor who is skeptical. The next time a new employee is hired or a regular employee is assigned to a new job, the Supervisor should jot down the time (hour and/or date) he is ready to go to work. Then the doubting Supervisor should note *when* that employee really became proficient on his job. How much time elapsed? How many errors did he make? How much work didn't he do? How much did this delay cost? The alternative to this is J.I.T., which cannot help but make sure that he is trained right the first time.

SOME SIMPLE SEMANTICS

Before we leave this introduction to J.I.T. and begin a careful examination of this method of teaching responsible people to teach others, two simple words need some clarification in connection with the work of this chapter.

1. **Position** is defined as the person's occupational title; e.g.: secretary, salesperson, deliveryman, etc.

2. **Job** is used primarily to denote one of the tasks or duties, the sum total of which make up the whole position; e.g.: the salesperson not only sells, but his position includes such other jobs as stockkeeping,

wrapping, taking cash, etc. In some instances, however, it is possible to interchange the words "job" and "position" because the position has only one job or task assigned to it; e.g.: cashier only takes cash; wrapper only packs merchandise; etc.

HOW J.I.T. WORKS

In the literature of the personnel and training field, J.I.T. is frequently referred to as the *four-step method* which this writer firmly believes to be a poor definition, and one that is quite incorrect. This opinion is based squarely on the facts: there actually five steps!

1. The Instructor Gets Ready to Teach
2. Prepare The Worker to Learn
3. Present the Job to the Worker
4. Try-out Performance
5. Follow-up

1. The Instructor Gets Ready to Teach

Good training, like any other good job performance, does not just *happen*. It must be planned. And the planning should be based upon sound and effective techniques of instructing and learning. Therefore, in getting ready to teach a job, the instructor should do the following.

a. **Have a Timetable**

Know when the employee will be taught.

TRAINING TIMETABLE

Name _____
Division _____
or
Section _____
Date _____

EMPLOYEES

Operations — Tasks

REMARKS

Submitted by _____ Checked _____

Know how much time the instructor and the learner have available.

Know how much you expect the learner to know and by what time or date.

b. Have Everything Ready

The right equipment.

The right materials.

The right supplies.

c. Have the Place Properly Arranged

Know *where* you want to teach.

Have all the material properly arranged so that no time is lost in looking for things.

If possible, teach the job in the place where the work will actually be done.

d. Break Down the Job

This is the most important part of the instructor's preparation. It is at this point that J.I.T.'s superiority as a teaching technique begins to assert itself. All too often, a Supervisor or a Sponsor or any untrained instructor, because he is experienced and familiar with the job, attempts to teach an employee how to do a job without first thinking of it from the viewpoint of the new worker. The

Supervisor (or instructor) often overlooks the fact that the newcomer has to pay attention to many small, simple things that he is *not* accustomed to doing. Thus, when the instructor takes some points for granted because the job he is teaching is so familiar to him that he frequently does it automatically, he leaves gaps in his instruction — gaps which the learner will find difficult to bridge by himself.

This part of the preparatory step of J.I.T. prevents all the above from happening. By being forced to *break down the job,* the instructor is able to see it through the eyes of the trainee and must present it to the learner step by step.

The best way for a Supervisor to *break down the job* is to sit down with paper and pencil and analyze the job with the problems of the learner in mind. This method is called the "Job Breakdown" and it is done on a simple "Job Breakdown Sheet." It involves putting down on paper the important steps in the specific job operation and the order in which they appear and should be learned. The instructor is asking himself: "What do I do first, then what is second, etc.?" The job breakdown is thus really no more than a series of notes that the instructor is making to himself. This is done (1) to describe the operation in a logical, *sequential* fashion — first things first and "why" things are done this way; (2) to avoid the natural tendency to teach too much; (3) to help the instructor remember important details which he might overlook because he knows the job too well; and (4) to make certain that he teaches the learner one step at a time.

JOB BREAKDOWN SHEET

PART _____ OPERATION _____

IMPORTANT STEPS IN THE OPERATION	KEY POINTS
Step: A logical segment of the operation when something is done to advance the work	Key Point: Anything in a step that might: Make or break the job. Injure the worker. Make the work easier to do. ("knack" "trick" special timing, bit of information)

Note that there are *"Steps"* and *"Key Points."*

"Steps" are the operations which are necessary to complete the job — in order of performance.

"Key Points" are what the instructor must remember to emphasize to the learner.

As we begin the actual instruction process part of J.I.T., it must be made clear to the reader what has been inferred up to now: J.I.T. is an individualized method of training — one instructor teaching a job to one learner at a time. It is not meant for training classes or groups.

2. **Prepare the Worker to Learn**

Before the actual physical instruction begins, it is sound educational practice to prepare the employee's mind for new ideas. The following are some of the things the instructor can do to prepare the worker to learn:

a. Put the employee at ease; make small talk about any timely topics. People who are nervous and tense do not learn as well as relaxed people.

b. Tell the employee what the objective of this instruction is, what the instructor plans to teach him and why.

c. Motivate the employee; make him feel important (avoid flattery). Tell him how important the job is and what it can do for him. (Better earnings? Promotional possibilities? etc.)

d. Tell the employee how this job fits into the overall picture — after telling him what is to be taught and why, it is considered good form "to show him the big picture."

    e. Find out what the employee already knows about the job — it makes good sense to make use of old ideas and skills if they are applicable. If they conflict with the current job, now is the time to urge the employee to discard them.

    f. Place the learner in the correct position — make sure that he can see and hear everything. Be certain that he is correctly placed to do the job when that phase is reached.

3. Present the Job to the Worker

    a. *Tell* the learner about the job — one step at a time, slowly and clearly.

    b. *Show* (demonstrate to) the learner *how* to do the job one step at a time, slowly and clearly, stressing the "KEY POINTS."

OR

    c. Where possible, tell and show at the same time, clearly and slowly, *one step at a time*, stressing "KEY POINTS."

    d. Do not present at one time more than the learner seems able to master.

    e. Stress repeating the "tell" and "show," when and if necessary.

    f. Set as high a standard as possible, make up your

mind that you will only be satisfied by the best performance possible. Don't be satisfied by an average job performance.

4. **Try-out Performance**

   a. Have the trainee *do* the job under your supervision, applying the information just given.

   b. Have the learner *do* the job over and over again, as many times as necessary to get the skills needed and until it seems certain that the learner has the job down pat.

   c. Have the employee *tell* and *show* what is to be done, as the instructor did in Step 3 (above). The learner should try to teach the instructor, step-by-step, stressing the "KEY POINTS" to the instructor. This is a testing device to make certain that he knows the job.

   d. The instructor should observe the learner closely to make sure that he understands what he is doing, and why. If necessary, the teacher should repeat some of the instruction.

   e. Correct any errors as they occur — reteach if necessary. If the instructor can catch an error at the beginning, a bad habit can be prevented.

5. **Follow-up**

   a. Put the employee on his own — let him do the job alone.

   b. Tell him where or to whom to go for advice.

- **c.** Check his work frequently, encourage questions, be critical, if necessary.

- **d.** Taper off observation and follow-up, gradually.

- **e.** Correct any new errors or bad habits or shortcuts that might crop up after the original instruction. Point out any weaknesses.

- **f.** Commend the employee for good performance and a job well done.

SUMMARY

J.I.T. is a "guaranteed," successfully proven method by which a beginner may be taught a job by someone delegated to teach that job. It consists of these simple steps.

Step 1: The Instructor Gets Ready to Teach

Step 2: The Learner is Prepared to Receive the Instruction

Step 3: The Instructor Presents the Job

Step 4: The Learner Applies What Has Been Taught

Step 5: Follow Up

"If the Instructor Has Taught, the Worker Can Perform."

Recommended Reading

Beckman: How To Train Supervisors — pp. 27-29

Craig and Bittel: Training and Development Handbook — pp. 11-12

Chapter Fourteen

Employee Evaluation

No matter what the work place or work situation may be, we are always forming opinions about the people around us. We are constantly *appraising* the people who work with us and *evaluating* their performance. As soon as a Supervisor meets his subordinates, he begins to "size them up," and he continues this process of informal evaluation throughout his relationship with them. There are those personnel management authorities who believe that this informal evaluation, even though it is casual and "off-the-cuff," is the natural way to handle this supervisory task. However, the overwhelming opinion holds to a more formal, definitive method of *rating* employees for many reasons on both the part of the employee and the company. This chapter, therefore, will concern itself entirely with *formal* employee evaluation and the communication to the employee of the evaluation in the form of merit ratings.

WHAT IS EMPLOYEE EVALUATION?

There are many complicated definitions of *what* employee evaluation is or means, but as always, the simplest one is probably the best one. It may be stated accordingly that employee evaluation is the system, process or method of determining which employees are succeeding on their jobs and which employees are doing poorly or failing. We will also discuss *why* as the introduction to this chapter seemed to indicate, there are a number of synonomous terms for this process of employee evaluation.

The literature of the field (and a great deal has been written about it), also refers to this measurement of job performance as employee *appraisal*, performance *rating*, merit *rating*, service *rating*, job *review*, and efficiency *rating*. We will use all these terms interchangeably although we can narrow or delimit the terms somewhat for our own purposes. Let us call the overall process employee evaluation or appraisal. As a result of a regularly-scheduled, systematic, impartial review of the employee's performance, a merit rating form is completed which summarizes the Supervisor's evaluation of each employee. From this written rating form, some action affecting the ratee's job may take place. And finally, the employee meets with the Supervisor or some other designated executive to discuss this performance appraisal.

It should be noted here that the employee evaluation should include a number of factors, some of which can be measured quite accurately and some of which can only be determined by means of the Supervisor's opinions and observations. These factors will be examined in detail later in this chapter.

WHY EVALUATE?

There are many reasons for instituting and maintaining a formal employee evaluation system. Among the following uses are those which indicate that they are valuable to the Supervisor or the company; others are beneficial to the employee:

1. Ratings are the principal means of determining the granting or denial of *salary increases,* both periodic and on merit. As a matter of fact, in too many organizations, this has become the only important reason for the use of the evaluation system. In one large department store, for example, a relative newcomer was advised by an oldtimer (much as an older sister advises a younger child around Christmas time) to be on her best behavior to make a good impression on her Supervisors because "it's rating time again."

2. Ratings can be used as an important consideration in *promotions,* particularly if the employee has consistently shown excellent ratings.

3. A complete evaluation of the employee's abilities and attitudes may serve as the means of pointing out to the Supervisor that a *transfer* may be in order.

   For example, in rating a salesperson, the Department Head may come to the conclusion that while the employee involved has fine attributes, her sales production and related factors indicate quite clearly that she is not "sales material." Accordingly, on the basis of the analytical features of the rating process, the Supervisor may decide to recommend a transfer to a non-selling department.

4. When sales are slow or production is at a low ebb, reduction of the force (R.O.F.) or *layoff* is usually necessary. If there is no seniority system involved, it would seem plausible for the Supervisor to retain the best workers as indicated by the employee evaluation system.

5. The most powerful weapon the Supervisor possesses is the power of *dismissal* or the recommendation thereof. In addition to the several causes for dismissal arising from disciplinary reasons, it is logical to expect that poor or consistently unsatisfactory work as reflected by his ratings can also bring about the employee's dismissal.

6. With the spread and growth of *unions*, the use of the evaluation system in labor-management dealings has come to the fore. Under the normal union contract, the power to dismiss for cause, or to otherwise severely discipline rank-and-file workers, is curtailed. The dismissal or other economic penalty must be concurred with by the union officials. Where the union will not agree, the normal procedure is to submit the matter to arbitration. A hearing is held in a quasi-judicial atmosphere. The arbitrator usually requires "evidence" that can stand up under legal scrutiny, and a well-organized employee evaluation system can provide just that. (See "How To Evaluate" which follows later.)

7. A well-planned, carefully-executed employee evaluation system can be very useful in revealing, by an analysis of the evaluation data, how effective the company's various *training programs* are. Poor ratings on any one item may require a revision of the training program as it affects that item.

8. Generally speaking, an employee likes to know how he is *doing* and where he *stands*. The evaluation system with its built-in merit-rating interview does just that on both counts.

9. When the employee knows how he is doing because the employee evaluation system shows him just that in fine detail, he can then do something to *improve* himself, if necessary.

10. The employee evaluation system does a good job, in general, for management, too. It keeps the employee on his toes, thereby helping to sustain or improve production (sales).

WHO SHOULD EVALUATE?

It is quite obvious that *who* is to do the rating or evaluation is a simple matter: the immediate Supervisor of the person to be rated or reviewed is most familiar with the employee's work, is in continuous touch with him, and can readily observe his job performance. The best minds in the field feel, however, that it is better to secure more than one rating on each employee. This is fine where there is more than one Supervisor who has the necessary knowledge about, and contact with, the ratee. For example, in those merchandising departments where there is a buyer, an assistant buyer, and/or a Section or Service Manager, we have an ideal situation which can lead to the formation of an appraisal committee. One principle must be kept in mind at all times in the determination of *who* is to do the rating: the rater must always be at least a first-line Supervisor. People on the same level must never rate one another; neither may the rank-and-file rate a Supervisor.

WHEN TO EVALUATE

The timing and frequency of the ratings will vary from organization to organization and from job to job within an organization. The variation may range from quarterly to semi-annually to annually. But the *usual* schedule for many positions in many firms is every six months. Firms which are unionized, however, have a special problem. The normal union-coverage clause in most contracts requires the new employee to join the union after a probationary period. Here again there is a great deal of variation since these probationary periods range from 15 to 180 days, with 30 days being the usual period. During the probationary period the company must determine whether to keep the newcomer or let him go. Once the probationary period has ended and the employee has joined the department as a full-time staff member, it is virtually impossible to separate the employee from the roster because of the typical union's attitude toward agreeing to a dismissal. Accordingly, firms that are unionized feel compelled to evaluate their new employees one or more times *before* the probation ends. Most companies, incidentally, rate their executives as well as their rank-and-file employees. In some companies middle-management executives are rated annually, while in others they, too, are evaluated semiannually.

HOW TO EVALUATE

Employee evaluation is frequently made synonymous with the appearance of a rating sheet or an appraisal from which summarizes the employee's performance. But if that is all employee evaluation means, it is doomed to failure. Therefore, it is well for the student to understand what *should* go into the production of this form. If the Supervisor merely sits down and checks off the qualities or characteristics contained therein, the evaluation will be perfunctory and of little value to either the employee and the company. It is important, therefore, that thoughtful consideration be given to the creation of a good system which is based upon: (1) records or objective statistics or information as well as opinions of the Supervisor(s) on (2) the employee's personal qualities and (3) job performance.

1. **Evaluation Based Upon Records or Objective Statistics or Information**

   There are a number of areas in any well-managed business from which the Supervisor (rater) can draw much meaningful information as to the progress and performance of the ratee:

   a. **Attendance records** which give an accurate picture of the employee's punctuality and regularity in attendance. See illustration on page 130.

   b. **Production records** in one form or another are kept or may be kept in almost all forms of business and for most jobs. For example, in selling, a salesperson's production may be determined by a simple ratio:

   $$\frac{\$ \text{ Employee's Salary}}{\$ \text{ Sales of Employee}} = \text{Selling Cost \%}$$

   Thus if a salesperson earns $60 per week and his sales for that week are $600, his selling cost percent is 10%.

   (Salary ÷ Sales = Selling Cost %)

   $$\frac{\$60}{\$600} = 10\%$$

EMPLOYEE ATTENDANCE RECORD

Week Ending	ABSENCES Personal	ABSENCES Hospital	LATES Arrival	LATES Lunch	LATES Failure to Clock	SUPERVISORS' RECORD OF INTERVIEWS Enter pertinent comments, (Please print), date of interview and signature
1- 2						
1- 9						
1-16						
1-23						
1-30						
2- 6						
2-13						
2-20						
2-27						
3- 6						
3-13						
3-20						
3-27						
4- 3						
4-10						
4-17						
4-24						
5- 1						
5- 8						
5-15						
5-22						
5-29						
6- 5						
6-12						
6-19						
6-26						

Enter initial for days of week up to 5 in absence column.
Indicate in absence column, if employee was on vac., leave of absence or M.MA.
Check (√) if attendance is perfect.
Enter N.T.C. if time card is missing and follow up with timekeeper.

F. 1271A—3-53

The sales Supervisor will know if 10 percent is considered a good sales ratio depending upon previous experience, the time of the year, etc.

Production data can be accumulated for all types of jobs and the individual employee's performance measured to an average production figure.

PERSONNEL REVIEW

Quarter Ending	GROSS SALES	CREDITS AMOUNT	CREDITS IND. %	CREDITS DEPT. %	NET SALES	Am't. of Sal. Earned	TRANS.	SELLING COST IND. %	SELLING COST DEPT. %
Apr.									
July									
Oct.									
Jan.									
Apr.									
July									
Oct.									
Jan.									
Apr.									
July									
Oct.									
Jan.									
Apr.									
July									

c. **Error records** are kept by many firms. In some places these may be called *damage records*. For example, department stores generally find it important to prevent errors, particularly in sending

131

merchandise to customers, and they have instituted "error systems" which record all types of mistakes made by salespeople. Frequent errors, or a greater number of errors than the average person in the department, can form the basis of retraining as well as a performance standard.

ERROR
RETURN FOR CORRECTION

DETECTED BY DEPT.–CLERK	SALESCHECK DATE	ERROR BY DEPT.–CLERK	SALESBOOK AND CHECK NO.
—		—	—
DATE			

TYPE OF ERROR	WRONG	OMITTED	INCOMPLETE	TYPE OF ERROR	WRONG	OMITTED	INCOMPLETE
1. Salescheck Information	xx	xx	xx	**4. Customer's Name and Address:**	xx	xx	xx
a. Date, Dept., Clerk No.				a. Illegible			
b. Chg. or Amt. Recd., Kind of Sale				b. First and Last Full Names			
c. Customer's Sig., S/M Authorization, Release No., Cash Authorization				c. Complete House No. and Street Name or No.			
d. Cash Equivalent Info.				d. Full City or Borough Name			
2. Merchandise:	xx	xx	xx	e. Abbreviation for State Name			
a. Quantity, Style, Size, Color, No. of Pieces				f. Apartment No.			
b. Damaged, Soiled, Incomplete				**5. Special Instructions:**	xx	xx	xx
3. Amount of Sale:	xx	xx	xx	a. Enclosures			
a. Unit Price				b. Gift Wrap			
b. Extension				c. Future Delivery			
c. Total Amount of Sale				d. Others (New Worn— Own Sent)			
d. Shipping Charges				**6. Heldover Salescheck Not Approved**			
e. Tax (City-Federal)				**7. Other**			

REMARKS

SALESCLERK'S SIGNATURE | **SECTION MANAGER'S SIGNATURE**

CARELESSNESS CAUSES COMPLAINTS

F.1116 50M 4-50 B.P.

d. **Returns** (for merchandising or sales organizations) may be regarded as an adjunct to error or damage records. Where wholesale or retail customers are involved some amount of "returns" must be expected. But a constant high level of returned goods by unsatisfied customers may be symptomatic of poor salesmanship.

e. **Customer's opinions** (for merchandising or sales organizations) can be another important factor in evaluating relatively objective data in the appraisal process. Customers' opinions may come from the following sources:

1. Letters of complaint or commendation.

2. Verbal complaints or commendation expressed to adjustment or managerial personnel.

f. **Service Shopping** (for retailing firms) by outside, professional organizations has been developed into big business in all parts of the country by such firms as Willmark, Merit, Dale, etc. Some stores use new people such as executive trainees as shoppers for a short time; a few companies employ clubwomen who donate their fees to their favorite charity.

Service shopping, either done by professionals or amateurs, operates in a similar fashion: the company arranges to have people posing as regular customers who purchase goods and report their experiences with the salesperson involved on an objective service shopping report form. As an incidental factor, the employee's honesty in

Form 20

S. Q. B.
(Selling-Quotient-Builder)

S. Q. [   ]%

Company Name _____
Address _____
City _____ State _____

Quan.	Mdse. Purchased	Amt. Sale	Amt. Tend.

Date _____ Time _____ A.M. / P.M.
Dept. _____ Floor _____

DESCRIPTION OF SALESPERSON

Man ○ Woman ○   Sp's. No. or letter _____
Approximate Age _____ Build: Slender ○
Height _____   Medium ○
Color of hair _____   Heavy ○
Style of hair _____ Wearing glasses ○
Description of clothes _____
Special marks of identification _____

A—APPROACH TO CUSTOMER

	Yes	No	
1—Department Busy?	☐	☐	
2—Prompt Approach?	☐	☐	
3—If not prompt—			
a. Did sp. recognize you as waiting customer?	☐	☐	**3**
b. You waited aprox. ___ min.			
c. Reasonable delay	☐	☐	**3**
4—Sp's expression pleasant on approaching	☐	☐	**2**
5—Quote greeting			

VALUE 8

D—CREATING DESIRE FOR MDSE.

Was there any need to create desire or induce decision on purchased mdse.? ☐ Yes ☐ No
(If "No" do not answer Section "D")

	Yes	No	
1—Gave details on good qualities of mdse.?	☐	☐	**3**
2—Stressed benefits you would enjoy from mdse. in use	☐	☐	**3**
3—Justified price of mdse.	☐	☐	**2**
4—Answered questions satisfactorily	☐	☐	**3**

VALUE 11

G—APPEARANCE OF SALESPERSON

	Yes	No
1—Hair neat?	☐	☐
2—Clothing neat?	☐	☐
3—Fingernails clean?	☐	☐
4—Was salesperson—chewing gum— smoking on duty?—	○ ○	○ ○

VALUE 5

B—SECURING ATTENTION

1—Was requested mdse. in stock? ☐ ☐

2—If not, did sp. attempt to fill your requirements? ☐ ☐10
   a. Suggested a substitute ○
   b. Offered to order item ○
   c. Directed you to another dept. ○

3—Name item not in stock _____

VALUE 10

Did you voluntarily select all mdse. from a display ☐ ☐

(If "Yes" do not answer Section "C")

C—ESTABLISHING INTEREST

1—Was sp. familiar with location of stock? ☐ ☐2
   a. Familiar with prices? ☐ ☐2

2—Showed wide enough assortment of mdse. ☐ ☐3

3—Showed mdse. pleasingly ☐ ☐3

VALUE 10

E—TRADING UP

No opportunity to trade up ○

1—Made effort to trade up on requested mdse.? ☐ ☐12
   a. Offered larger size unit ○
   b. Better quality mdse. ○
   c. More than one of item ○

2—Actually showed this mdse. ☐ ☐2

3—Stressed benefits to be enjoyed from more or better mdse. ☐ ☐2

VALUE 12

F—SUGGESTION SELLING

No opportunity to suggest ○

1—Suggested additional mdse. other than that requested ☐ ☐12

2—Did sp. show this mdse.? ☐ ☐2

3—Did sp. stress benefits of buying suggested mdse.? ☐ ☐2

4—Quote suggestion _____

VALUE 12

H—APPEARANCE OF DEPARTMENT

1—Floor clean? ☐ ☐
2—Mdse. neatly arranged? ☐ ☐1
3—Dept. well lighted? ☐ ☐
4—Mdse. clean and fresh? ☐ ☐   **VALUE 1**

I—COMPLIANCE WITH STORE SYSTEM

1—System used—Register ○   Book ○   Cert. ○

2—If register used, was drawer
   Closed ○   Could not observe ○   Open │○3

3—If system calls for receipt to customer—
   Was receipt given on above purchase? ☐ ☐8

4—Was merchandise given to you—
   After you paid ○   Before you paid ○6

5—Did salesperson call back—
   Amt. sale ☐ ☐2
   Amt. tend. ☐ ☐2
   Change ☐ ☐2
   No change required ○

6—Did sp. give you mdse. and change without unusual delay? ☐│☐2

VALUE 25

J—CLOSING OF SALE

1—What did sp. say at close? _____

Said nothing at close   │○6

VALUE 6

ADD NUMBERS LISTED BESIDE "NO" SQUARES AND CIRCLES IN WHICH X MARKS APPEAR. SUBTRACT TOTAL FROM 100, GIVING YOU THE S.Q. PERCENTAGE.

Remarks _____

handling cash and store systems is also checked by the shopper. Service shopping, if done regularly and properly, can add valuable information to the recorded information available for employee evaluation.

2. **Evaluating Personal Qualities**

   An employee's total job performance may very well be affected by the extent to which he possesses personal qualities such as enthusiasm, initiative, patience and tact, cooperation, reliability, interest, etc. Obviously, these personal qualities are hard to record and still more difficult to measure. It is important, therefore, that those whose job it is to evaluate be trained and thoroughly impressed with the necessity of being as impartial and objective as possible.

3. **Evaluating Job Performance**

   While there must be some variation in the factors arising from the evaluation of job performance, there is general agreement on most of the following criteria:

   a. **Appearance** — including adherence to dress regulations, cleanliness, grooming, etc.

   b. **Accuracy** — particularly in handling numbers, cash, and the use of systems and procedures, etc.

   c. **Knowledge** — can mean such things as merchandise or stock knowledge, skills, etc.

   d. **Quality of work** — takes into account such factors

as accuracy and completeness of the work done, etc.

e. **Quantity of work** — is synonymous with volume of work — how rapidly and consistently the work is done, etc. Using the three different types of information discussed above, a rating scale may be constructed which can best serve the interests of the company. See illustration on page 138.

Using the appraisal form provided and the data available, the Supervisor(s) may proceed to rate the employees under their supervision. Where there is more than one Supervisor rating each individual, a consensus may be made of each employee's rating.

THE RATING INTERVIEW

In concluding this chapter on employee evaluation, we have left the most important consideration for last. All of the preceeding words and ideas are worthless if nothing further is done. It is difficult to imagine large business organizations who do all we have analyzed and discussed up to now and then end the evaluation process with the completed rating form safely tucked in the employee's personnel file. In other words, all this work never sees the light of day in some companies — it is regarded as "confidential." It is almost unbelievable that such a situation can and does exist in the business world.

It would seem ridiculously obvious that unless the rating is thoroughly discussed with each employee by the rater it can be of little service.

Fortunately, most firms do insist on a rating or appraisal interview which adheres to the following general pattern:

SALES MANAGER PERFORMANCE APPRAISAL

Instructions:

Indicate your judgment of this executive by checking the most applicable rating for each of the factors listed below. If because of limitation of time in position, or other reasons, factor cannot be appraised, state "cannot rate" and reason. The ratings are defined as follows:

OUTSTANDING	– Noticeably exceeds requirements of position
VERY GOOD	– More than adequately meets requirements of position
SATISFACTORY	– Adequately meets requirements of position
BELOW STANDARD	– Does not adequately meet requirements of position

DUTIES

Indicate to what degree the executive performs the following:

	OUT-STANDING	VERY GOOD	SATIS-FACTORY	BELOW STANDARD

I. SERVICE SUPERVISION

1. Exemplifies high service standards in his contacts with customers.
2. Ensures that waiting customers are served at point of sale.
3. Provides adequate service at wrapping and cashiering stations.
4. Opens and closes department efficiently and on time.
5. Provides salesclerks with up-to-date information on availability of merchandise, new merchandise, advertised items, delivery dates, special orders and new policies and procedures.
6. Resolves complaints in accordance with Macy's adjustment policy.
7. Schedules sales and stock employees to provide coverage when needed, at minimum expense.
8. Maintains a clean, orderly and safe work area.
9. Ensures that stubbing and tallying procedures are properly followed.
10. Requires strict adherence to salescheck and sales register procedures.
11. Adheres to time schedules established for all reports including volume, counts, reorders, requisitions, want slips, complaint jackets, etc.
12. Achieves sales goals.

II. MERCHANDISE SUPERVISION

13. Arranges, signs and maintains attractive and timely merchandise displays.
14. Maintains prescribed merchandise assortments by adhering to count schedules, supervising counts and requisitioning merchandise.
15. Controls the movement of "AS IS," prior and salvage merchandise and disposes of it promptly.
16. Is alert to customer demand for merchandise not carried.
17. Responds to customer demand for seasonal merchandise by making appropriate changes in merchandise presentation.
18. Recommends changes in model stocks, assortment lists and basic items.
19. Takes price changes accurately and promptly.
20. Enforces the shortage reduction program for his area.
21. Plans and executes semi-annual inventory.

III. PERSONNEL AND COMMUNICATIONS

22. Is fair, friendly and businesslike in the treatment of subordinates.
23. Informs employees of required standards of performance.
24. Trains and develops employees.
25. Provides employees with the physical facilities necessary to perform their duties.
26. Cooperates with and maintains continuing two way communications with subordinates, superiors and executives on his own level.
27. Makes effective use of his own time.
28. Observes and requires adherence to Company rules and systems

Performance Review of: _____
(Name)

Identification Number |_|_|_|_|_|_|

Location Number |_|_|_|_|_|_|

Date Employed by Macy Corp.: _____

Date of Present Assignment: _____

Review Covers Period From: _____ To: _____

Administrator or Vice Pres.: _____

REASONS

Explain, where significant, how the employee can improve. If below standard, give specific reasons for the rating.

OBJECTIVES FOR NEXT YEAR

What are your joint objectives for next year?

1. The Supervisor prepares for the interview by:

    a. Securing a place for the interview which will insure privacy.

    b. Arranging a time that is mutually convenient.

    c. Having available copies of the employee's past ratings to be able to show improvement or lack of it.

    d. Producing any records or data which may be pertinent to support the current rating.

2. As the interview begins the first task of the Supervisor should be to ease the tension and relieve the anxiety that may be present, and generally to put the ratee at ease. Since the primary purpose of the appraisal interview may be likened to a training session because the employee may need to learn ways and means of improving himself, the atmosphere most conducive to learning is one where tension is absent.

3. If the employee is new and has never been evaluated before and has never been present at a rating interview, the Supervisor should discuss briefly the purpose of both the interview and the rating process. If the employee is aware of the purpose of the interview, it is only necessary for the Supervisor to make some casual remarks about the occasion.

4. At this point, the Supervisor should either pause briefly to give the ratee a chance to ask questions, or ask the employee if he has any questions thus far.

5. Now, for the first time, the Supervisor should show the

employee his rating sheet and give him an opportunity to examine it. Opportunities for the ratee to ask questions about the rating should again be allowed at this point. However, the Supervisor must be certain to control the interview and not to permit the ratee to protest items on which he may have been rated poorly. If this occurs, the Supervisor need only indicate that there will be sufficient opportunity to discuss the rating in detail.

6. It is considered good psychology and wise management technique to start the detailed discussion by presenting those points on the rating scale which are complimentary and in which the ratee has excelled. Everyone likes to feel that effort and/or performance is recognized by a higher authority, and in the dialogue that may follow, the employee may frequently voice his appreciation for the recognition accorded him by the evaluation of his good attributes.

7. If there are nothing but good points on the rating scale, the interview can practically come to a close at this point; but if there is a mixture of excellent and satisfactory scores, the rater may feel it important to urge the employee to try to raise the level of his rating the next time around so that all of the criteria may be judged as excellent.

8. In many instances, however, this part of the rating interview may well be considered the highlight because it should be used to point out where the employee is *weak,* or perhaps even failing to meet acceptable standards of performance.

9. The Supervisor should be prepared at this point for the natural reaction on the part of any employee to alibi,

defend, or excuse himself. There will also be an opportunity here for female employees to shed a few tears. If the Supervisor understands human nature, he will give the employee every opportunity to react naturally.

10. When the employee appears to have finished with the excuses, alibis and tears, the Supervisor should gently turn the discussion to more constructive ways by which the ratee might seek to improve the weak points indicated on the rating scale.

11. Wherever possible, the Supervisor should seek to have the ratee find his own solution for each weak point. Of course, the rater may assist him by pointing out ways and means of improvement where necessary. The interview should not head towards a close unless or until the employee thoroughly understands what is expected of him and the things he must do in order to eliminate those aspects of the appraisal form on which he is now rated as unsatisfactory or failing.

12. It would be obviously unfair to the employee if another six months were to go by without a re-evaluation of those areas on the evaluation form in which the interview has sought improvement by the employee. Accordingly, the Supervisor should set a date in the immediate future to re-open the discussion, if necessary, but to assess primarily the extent of the improvement which is expected to follow in this merit rating interview.

13. The Supervisor's final task in this patterned interview comes at a later date when he begins to follow up and to look for the improvement in the ratee's work as discussed above.

14. If the improvement is not forthcoming or, if the Supervisor deems that sufficient improvement has not occurred, it is expected that he will counsel the employee further. Or, if the Supervisor decides that the lack of improvement is deliberate, he may find it necessary to reprimand the employee or even put him on probation. If this is the case, more follow-up will obviously be necessary in the immediate future.

15. If in the course of the follow-up the Supervisor is able to discern real improvement, he should make it his business to compliment the employee and to encourage him even further.

While it may seem to the student that this chapter on Employee Evaluation has taken up a great deal of time and space for a supervisory duty which only occurs several times a year, the writer should like once again to point out that, in effect, the evaluation job is a continuous one, and that the conscientious Supervisor is actually taking almost six months of daily appraisal and evaluation to do the job right.

Recommended Reading

Ecker, MacRae et al: Handbook for Supervisors – Chapter 9

Flippo: Principles of Personnel Management – Chapter 15

Halsey, G. D.: Supervising People – Chapter 12

Dooher and Marquis: Effective Communication on the Job – pp. 153-164

Sartain and Baker: The Supervisor and His Job – Chapter 21

Chapter Fifteen

Giving Orders

In the first chapter of this book, supervision was simply and clearly defined as: "Getting work done through people." It follows, therefore, that the Supervisor, in getting his work accomplished, must continually give orders. It also goes without saying that the way he gives those orders will determine how successful a Supervisor he will be.

There is no simple formula for giving effective orders because there are so many factors involved. One factor concerns how experienced or perceptive the worker receiving the order is. Some employees need a detailed explanation of what to do; others need only a brief word or motion to do the same job.

WHAT TO CONSIDER IN GIVING ORDERS

While managers agree that it is difficult to generalize about giving orders, they also agree that there are definite points to observe when giving orders that they expect to be carried out. Some of these requisites for effective order-giving include:

1. The Supervisor giving the order should be thoroughly familiar with the job to be done, and generally capable of doing it himself, if necessary.

2. The employee receiving the order should be able to *do it* because he has the training, skill and physical and mental ability necessary.

3. The order should be given by the Supervisor in a clear, concise manner, speaking distinctly and using language (technical or otherwise) which is not too far above the employee's understanding nor too low to be insulting. Avoiding sarcasm or profanity, his orders should be expressed in a positive rather than a negative fashion.

4. The Supervisor should not give too many orders at one time. Trying to do too much frequently leads to none of the orders being carried out correctly.

5. The Supervisor should not take it for granted that the worker understands the order, but must make sure that it is understood. This can be done not only by directly asking the employee if he really understands what is expected of him, but also by asking the worker to repeat the order or to tell it back. In fact, it is generally a good practice for the Supervisor to *repeat* the order. Repetition is, after all the oldest and best teacher.

6. In some cases, the Supervisor will find it practical to demonstrate — to *show* how he wants the order carried out.

7. The Supervisor should avoid overloading the employee

by assigning more work by one order than the employee can actually do. In the same vein, the Supervisor should allow a reasonable amount of time for the job to be done.

8. Some orders should be put in writing, particularly if they are complicated. (This will be discussed in a later section of this chapter.)

9. The Supervisor should give orders through proper channels and not violate lines of authority by either by-passing an immediate Supervisor or by telling another worker to give someone on his own level — a peer — the order to do a job.

10. The worker should be *motivated* to be willing to do the job implicit in the order. Whenever practical, the worker should be shown *how* he can benefit. It is also a good idea to explain *why* the order is necessary, whenever possible.

11. Once the order is given, the Supervisor should show confidence in the employee and not stand over him, urging or nagging him to finish the work.

12. Follow up after allowing a reasonable time for the work to begin and to progress. Correct any errors or commend the worker if the work is going along well.

WAYS OF GIVING ORDERS

In addition to a knowledge of the prerequisites for effective order-giving, the executive must also be aware of the various *methods* of giving an order. Orders generally fall into four classifications:

1. **The request order** should be used for most order-giving. It is in complete accord with the current human relations thinking in industry and emphasizes the "treat others as you would like to be treated" attitude that is so essential today. Frequently, but not mandatorily, the request order will take the form of a question such as:

    "Will you do this next, please?"

    "How about doing this?"

    "I wonder if you would like to do this?"

    Usually the word "please" is part of the request or question. The new or young Supervisor need have little worry or fear that the employee will respond to the request or question by saying: "No, I would *not* like to do that." Such a refusal is tantamount to insubordination and is generally a cause for dismissal.

    In addition to its "universal" appeal, the request order should *always* be used for giving orders to the older person, the sensitive, touchy employee, the new employee, and by one Supervisor to another.

2. **The direct order or "command"** should generally be avoided, since it is out of keeping with the current democratic spirit in employee-employer relations; it is a relic of the day when the boss was an autocrat in every sense of the word. Today, except for just a few "legitimate" reasons, all the direct order does effectively is arouse resentment and bad feeling. However, it is perfectly proper for the Supervisor to use the direct order in dealing with a lethargic employee — it may rudely awaken or shock him into realization that his job may be at stake; and it is certainly mandatory for use in

an emergency situation where instant action or obedience is required.

The direct order is easily recognizable by its commanding expressions:

"Do this."

"Get that."

"Move those . . ."

3. **The suggested or implied order** is a relatively unimportant type of order-giving compared to the request order. But it is an interesting aspect of supervisory technique and one towards which the alert, intelligent young executive may well seek to aspire. In using the implied order, the Supervisor "suggests" or "implies" that something needs to be done. For example, the buyer who observes that the selling floor is messed up and requires immediate stock-keeping attention may remark: "My, but we have been busy making sales this morning"; or the manager may muse aloud: "We are running behind schedule. I wonder if we will be able to finish the work."

This type of order is intended to stimulate initiative and develop responsibility among experienced workers. It should be noted that there must also be present a good sense of rapport between Supervisor and employees that may engender the use of such suggestions in place of an order.

4. **Asking for volunteers** is a challenging if infrequently used form of order-giving. In contrast to the request or direct order, the call for a volunteer to do a job is not

really an order, but since it is being used to get something done, it needs to be discussed here. It may be used to get a job done that is either dirty, dangerous, or disagreeable, but primarily it is used in the ordinary work day for securing personnel to work overtime, a normally unpopular assignment.

As a practical measure, the use of volunteers can serve a good purpose. It affords an employee who wishes to volunteer the chance to seek and acquire a measure of recognition he feels he needs for his own sense of well-being and security from the Supervisor and the group. The Supervisor, on the other hand, really has nothing to lose; if he does not get a volunteer, he may always fall back on a request or direct order.

WRITTEN ORDERS

It is often necessary to follow one of the oldest adages of order giving: "Put it in writing." There are a number of situations where the Supervisor will find it advisable to use a written order instead of the customary verbal one:

1. If the order is complicated and has many details.

2. If the worker for whom the order is intended has a poor memory or a tendency to forget things.

3. If there are several numbers, such as dollars, sizes, units, etc., involved that are quite obviously impossible to convey by an oral order.

4. If either party to the order — the giver or the receiver — will not be present at the time the order-giving is necessary.

5. When it is felt necessary or important to hold the employee accountable for receiving the order and understanding its content.

The important thing for the Supervisor to remember about giving an order is that it is a means to an end — it is given to get results from his subordinates, and it should be regarded in that light.

Recommended Reading

A.M.A.: Leadership on the Job — pp. 63-67

Beckman: How To Train Supervisors — pp. 128-135

Dooher and Marquis: Effective Communication on the Job — pp. 97-101

Chapter Sixteen

Maintaining Discipline

Rules of conduct and behavior are essential no matter what type of organization, institution or group is involved. Otherwise the lack of control that must ensue can only cause anarchy and chaos to prevail. Thus, the Supervisor is one of those who must find means of keeping order and insuring good conduct — in other words, maintaining discipline. The student who thinks nothing of the normal discipline code in school finds it difficult to believe that in the business world there should even be a need to study or discuss the subject.

The author always made this section of his courses in Executive Leadership a game. His class helped him fill all the available blackboard space by listing scores of employees' actions that violated ordinary business practice or the firm's own rules.

The following is only a partial list of actions that may call for disciplinary action by the manager in his daily supervisory activities:

1. Gross insubordination — willfully refusing to obey orders.

2. Slowdown.

3. Sabotage — deliberately destroying merchandise or supplies.

4. Stealing — money, merchandise, materials or supplies.

5. Drinking on the job; alcoholism; under the influence of liquor on the job.

6. Smoking — where prohibited.

7. Gambling — all forms.

8. Dangerous horseplay.

9. Immoral conduct or indecency.

10. Threatening, intimidating, or coercing fellow employees.

11. Leaving the premises without permission.

12. Making collections or donations without permission.

13. Circulating rumors — gossiping.

14. Taking too long for lunch or break(s).

15. Tardiness — including habitual lateness.

16. Absenteeism — including chronic absenteeism.

17. Wasting time — "goofing off."

18. Excessive talking — fooling around.

19. Fighting on the job — including assault.

20. Falsifying records, applications or reports.

21. Eating on the job.

22. Abuse of privileges — e.g., discount.

23. Improper dress for the job.

24. Discourteousness — being rude to the public.

25. Improper use of telephone.

Now that the potential manager has seen some of the places where employees can stray from the "straight and narrow path" of ordinary business conduct, we can proceed to analyze and discuss this problem briefly. There can be no question about the manager's willingness and ability to accept full responsibility for maintaining discipline; to surrender that responsibility means the Supervisor's abdicating of his job. The young Supervisor will generally find that most people readily obey reasonable rules of conduct or orders as long as they understand what is expected of them. The problem arises in the executive's dealings with the exceptions — those who do not or will not comply.

It is further interesting to note that where a Supervisor is lax in enforcing general discipline, even people who normally would not break the rules seem encouraged to do so. For example, the Department Head who does not discipline the first people who take more than the allotted time for the coffee break will soon find that not only is almost everyone "stretching his coffee break," but that the original uncorrected lapse of time has gradually become longer and longer. What is worse; if this is permitted to continue for any length of time at all, the employees will develop a feeling that they have acquired the right to do so.

It should be clear, therefore, that it is necessary, even vital, for the Supervisor to be fully aware of the discipline-maintenance function of his job. Now let us see what his course of action should be when a violation — any kind, by anyone — occurs within a Supervisor's jurisdiction. What should he do when he becomes aware of the infringement?

1. **He should move promptly but not hastily.** This does not mean that the Supervisor needs to mete out punishment at once, but it does mean that he should investigate if necessary. Inaction is tantamount to condoning the violation and may also breed resentment and insecurity. For example, Sally Brown, who works in the Infant's Wear Department, comes in late quite frequently. This day, she slipped in almost a half-hour late and thought that Martha Foster, her Department Head, did not notice her lateness because she did not do anything about it. By lunch time, Sally was sure she had "gotten away with it" and had nothing to worry about anymore.

However, Miss Foster did note the lateness but felt that she had more pressing problems; besides, it would do Sally good to "stew in her own juice" for a while. In mid-afternoon, when things were relatively quiet on the sales floor, Miss Foster got the Personnel Department's approval to discipline Sally Brown by "docking" her an hour's pay and suspending her without pay for the remaining two days of the week. Sally was, of course, very indignant because she had lulled herself into a sense of security. She would not have minded, she said loudly to all who would listen, "if she (Miss Foster) had had it out with me right then and there." Sally now has a real feeling of insecurity about Miss Foster. "I wonder what she is going to pull on me next?"

Prompt action means just that, or a *reasonable* facsimile. Anything else could engender more trouble than the delayed action is worth.

2. **He should get all the facts** necessary to handle the case. Of course, if the Supervisor sees the violation occurring before his very eyes, or hears it himself, doubt should not exist. Otherwise, the supervisor owes it to the employee involved to establish exactly what happened and why. Too frequently, the supervisor jumps to conclusions on only a fragment of the facts and an injustice to the worker may occur. In this incident Keith Gross, the buyer of the Men's Sportswear Department, collared Robert Smith, a salesman in his department, and demanded to know why he had been off the floor for one hour without permission. While Smith tried to explain, Mr. Gross ignored his attempts and continued to berate him, threatening to have him fired or transferred at the very least. When Smith finally got a word in edgewise, Mr. Gross discovered that Smith had been called to the office of the President of the store, in

his capacity as head of the store's American Legion Post, to go over the program for the Veterans' Day ceremonies at the store. Smith further explained that he had looked for Mr. Gross to tell him about the enforced absence, but unable to find him, he left word with the assistant buyer who had now also been called to the receiving room.

The Supervisor who leaps into disciplinary action without looking, often limps away in chagrin. Getting all the facts first obviates losing face with the whole department.

3. **He should keep cool and calm** regardless of the circumstances and/or the employee actions or attitudes. Frequently disciplinary situations tend to become emotional, especially for the employee to be "punished." In some instances, the Supervisor may envision the violation as an open defiance of both the rules and his position as Department Head, and this could arouse strong feelings in the Supervisor, too. Needless to say, disciplinary action (or any action, for that matter) which is done in the heat of anger or in a spirit of revenge is not to be trusted.

J. Laurence Bennett, brilliant young Advertising Manager of Robbins Mills, had acquired a new secretary, Miss Jody Merrill. Bennett found her a real delight as she quickly and smoothly took over the secretarial chores of his office. About one thing, however, J. L. Bennett was adamant — no one must ever disturb his desk. As a creative person, his desk always *seemed* to be littered and cluttered, but Bennett could find anything in a moment and without hesitation. One day, he came back unexpectedly from an overnight visit to the mill, which was in North Carolina. Miss Merrill, having caught up with all her work and with time on her hands, forgot the first-day warning not to disturb the J.L.B. desk. She was busily and happily engaged in tidying up "the mess." Mr. Bennett, on entering his private office and taking in the scene, flew into a towering rage. He shouted, hurled a few choice expletives, and in general, carried on like a madman. Poor Miss Merrill burst into tears and rushed from the room. When Bennett finally calmed down, he realized that he had made a mountain out of a molehill and that Miss Merrill was a rare gem in these days of careless, lackadaisical office help. He called her in, while she was in the midst of writing a note of resignation, apologized for his temper, and promised it would never happen again. When the atmosphere failed to return to normal, Mr. Bennett was forced to recommend Miss Merrill for a substantial salary increase to help assuage her feelings.

The Supervisor should always make it a rule to "cool off," not only to regain his composure but to have his emotions under full control in order to think logically and clearly.

4. **He should consider consulting others** if the infraction is a serious one which could invoke a severe penalty, such as dismissal. The obvious person to consult is the Supervisor's own immediate superior, who might eventually have to be involved anyway. If he feels the matter does not merit seeing his boss, the Supervisor could talk things over with and seek the advice of a colleague on the same level. Another consultation source is the Personnel Director or one of his aides.

5. **He should always be consistent** in the treatment of disciplinary offenses. This is a factor that is frequently ignored, particularly when the same offense is

committed by a favored (pet) employee. The cry of favoritism is serious and is one way for the Supervisor to lose the respect of most of his staff.

For example, William Bench, the Department Head, caught Sam Simon leaving the building without permission fifteen minutes before the end of the day. Normally, this infraction of the rules would cost Simon at least an hour's pay, possibly a day's suspension without pay, and certainly a severe reprimand. Because it was the week before Christmas, Bench merely "slapped Simon's wrist" and let him go scot-free. The rest of the staff members protested that Bench had penalized them for trying the same trick during the rest of the year. They said, Christmas or not, Simon should get the same treatment as anyone else.

The five principles stated above were derived from the good judgment and active usage of many top-notch Supervisors. If the young Supervisor considers them carefully, his decisions as to what to *actually do* in handling violations as they occur will be simplified. There are various penalties available to the Supervisor if the facts and the company's policies warrent the imposition of a penalty. Among the ways of disciplining workers are:

1. **Oral reprimand** — the most commonly used and most important form of discipline imposed on employees. (The reprimand will be dealt with separately and in detail later in this chapter.)

2. **Written reprimand** — is used primarily where there is a union involved. Most union contracts require the Supervisor to file a written reprimand, copies of which go to the employee, the union, and the Personnel Department of the company, to be made part of the

employee's record. Repeated written warnings such as these are cumulative and usually end in dismissal.

3. **Probation** — is the final reprimand that warns the employee that if the violation occurs again, some drastic action such as dismissal or suspension will almost automatically result.

4. **Restriction or denial of privileges** — parking, shopping on company time, the employee discount, breaks, use of the telephone, and salary advances are among the common privileges that may be lost or suspended for various infractions connected either with abusing the privilege itself or as a general form of penalty.

5. **Transfer** — to another department, another location or to another job — all with the implication that the new factor would be an undesirable move for the worker. Even if there were no overt undesirable effects, the mere change, involving leaving old friends and familiar working conditions to start anew, is often punishment enough.

6. **Deduction from pay (docking)** — is a common form of punishment for those who take too long for lunch or breaks, or for absence from work, in general.

7. **Demotion in rank** — should only be used in rare instances, particularly at the request of the employee who does not find his rank suitable, fitting or rewarding. It may also be used during times of economic recession when a cutback is necessary. In all other cases, demotion leaves a bitter, disillusioned and usually ineffective employee who can only cause trouble.

8. **Suspension or layoff without pay** — a severe economic

measure that can vary from a few hours to a month or more. The improperly attired employee for example, may be sent home for more suitable clothing and "docked" for the time missed. A severe infraction can bring several days' or weeks' suspension.

9. **Restricting opportunity for promotion or pay raise** — for an indefinite time. The Supervisor may tell the individual concerned that until he is sure that there will not be a recurrence of the infraction, he is withholding his needed approval of a pay raise or other form of promotion.

10. **Dismissal** — the strongest action possible as a punishment measure, it should be and usually is reserved for insubordination, felonious actions etc., or for habitual infractions of the company's rules.

These ten commonly used methods of disciplining workers are not push buttons on a console in the Supervisor's desk which he may press at will to have the penalty automatically dispensed. In the first place, there are many instances where it is necessary to make the penalties progressive in an ascending order of severity. Let us take the case of Sidonia Trueblood who came in late one morning. Her Supervisor Melvin Burke, the Manager of the Handbag Department, called the lateness to her attention in a mild manner since it was a first offense. When, soon after, Mr. Burke noticed Sidonia's next lateness, he called her aside and spoke gently but firmly to her about the evils of tardiness as a habitual offense. Several weeks later Sidonia was more than a half-hour late due to a train mishap, but Mr. Burke ordered her "docked" one hour's pay for this third offense, and again warned her. Sidonia's alarm clock failed her shortly thereafter and Mr. Burke not only "docked" her but gave her a probationary warning — the next time she was late was going to be her last day on the job. Unfortunately, this day came too soon and Sidonia found herself not only out of work but even unable to collect unemployment insurance because she was discharged for cause.

Another important consideration in taking specific disciplinary actions is *who* is being disciplined. Many employees are generally well-meaning and well-behaved, but they have occasional lapses in conduct. These people require some mild correction, but they do not constitute a real problem. While the Supervisor need not apologize for his action — usually a reprimand — neither does he have to be as severe as he would with the chronic or habitual offender.

THE REPRIMAND

With the exception of the most serious offenses such as felony violations (theft or assault), insubordination, and similar offenses where dismissal or other severe penalties must be invoked by the Supervisor in his daily efforts to retain decorum and order in his department, the reprimand is the tool most often employed in maintaining discipline. The following are some brief considerations involved in the use of the reprimand:

1. The Supervisor should investigate all actions and get all the facts before he uses it.

2. The Supervisor should be sure he has the right person and that this person deserves both the blame and the reprimand.

3. The Supervisor must be sure to reprimand in absolute privacy to protect the dignity of the individual.

4. The Supervisor should not delay the reprimand, but his promptness should not interfere with normal business activities.

5. The Supervisor should never use sarcasm, profanity, or abuse during the reprimand.

6. The Supervisor should tell the employee why he is being reprimanded — he should be specific and give the employee a chance to reply to the charges.

7. The Supervisor should be tactful but frank, firm and honest about the reprimand he is administering.

8. The Supervisor should never show favoritism by avoiding using the reprimand where it is deserved.

9. The Supervisor should never rub in the reprimand in a nasty way; neither should he ever strike, push or use any other physical means or gestures.

10. The Supervisor must show the employee how to avoid repeating the violation or the reprimand is a worthless gesture.

11. The Supervisor should never delegate the task of administering the reprimand to anyone not authorized to do so. This delegation should never be given to someone on the same level as the intended recipient of the reprimand.

12. The Supervisor should vary the depth and severity of the reprimand with the individual involved. He must never try to humiliate anyone by its use.

THE CORRECTIVE INTERVIEW

We have used terms such as "punishment," "disciplinary method or action," etc., in order to make the subject matter clear, bright and stark. But the human relations view of discipline is a positive one rather than the usually prevalent negative one. Modern supervisory techniques insist that maintaining discipline should be equated with training or retraining the errant worker. Accordingly, it is necessary in this final section of the chapter to discuss the discipline problem in terms of correcting the employee. Such retraining usually takes place at a "corrective" interview, and such a session should be made up of three parts:

1. Preparation by the Supervisor.

2. Conducting the corrective interview.

3. Follow-up by the Supervisor.

1. Preparation by the Supervisor.

a. The Supervisor should know as much about the employee as possible, especially if the Supervisor is new.

b. The Supervisor should know the job situation and the background for the needed correction.

c. The Supervisor should adopt the attitude that he will be firm but friendly during the interview.

d. The Supervisor should arrange a suitable, private place and a mutually convenient time for the corrective interview.

2. **Conducting the corrective interview.**

   a. The Supervisor should put the employee at ease and start in a pleasant way.

   b. The Supervisor should present the situation that needs correction in such a way as to focus the attention of the interview on the *error* and its *remedy* rather than on the employee.

   c. The Supervisor should try to get the employee to recognize the *error* himself and to suggest ways and means of correction.

   d. The Supervisor should assist the employee in finding the right solution, if necessary; but in any event, the interview should end on a note of encouragement.

3. **Follow-up by the Supervisor.**

   a. The Supervisor should act promptly on any decisions arising from the corrective interview.

   b. The Supervisor should mark his calendar for future reference as to further interviews, if necessary.

   c. The Supervisor should watch for improvement; he should commend if the improvement occurs and he should give more help or correction, if necessary.

   d. The Supervisor should check to see that everyone concerned has received proper attention, tying up any loose ends.

This chapter has attempted to focus the student's attention

on the need for maintaining effective discipline. A young Supervisor once complained that he felt like the Mikado in the famous Gilbert and Sullivan operetta, singing that famous refrain: "My object all sublime . . . to make the punishment fit the crime." It is true that while only a minute amount of the Supervisor's time is spent in dealing with disciplinary problems, "minute for minute, this can be the most important time he spends."

Recommended Reading

A.M.A.: Leadership on the Job — pp. 190-205

Beckman: How To Train Supervisors — pp. 158-163

Beach: Personnel: The Management of People at Work — Chapter 21

Dooher and Marquis: Effective Communication on the Job — pp. 104-107

Sartain and Baker: The Supervisor and His Job — Chapter 19

Chapter Seventeen

Handling Complaints and Grievances

When something bothers an employee or if he feels dissatisfied with some phase of his work, he may express his annoyance in the form of a *complaint*. When the condition or situation resulting in the employee's complaint is of a minor nature, it need not be a matter of major concern to the Supervisor. The Supervisor cannot afford, however, to let what may appear to him to be a minor complaint go completely unresolved. Any complaint, regardless of how minor it may seem, may reach the point where the employee feels an injustice has been dealt him. It is at this point that the Supervisor has a *grievance* on his hands.

There are bound to be complaints no matter how well a company or department is run, no matter how democratic the Supervisor may be, no matter how fine a spirit of human relations prevails. If these complaints are ignored or dealt with in an unfair or slipshod manner, they will, in almost every case, become grievances that may cause the Supervisor myriad problems.

It makes sense, therefore, for the alert, intelligent Supervisor to make every effort to prevent a simple annoyance or complaint from becoming a grievance. There are four important things a Supervisor can do to avoid the occurrence of grievances.

1. **The Supervisor should clear up minor annoyances** and complaints as they are expressed by the employee. The average worker is loathe to bother his boss, so when he does, the Supervisor should react accordingly and attempt to clear these small matters up. Delay only makes the employee brood, gripe to others, or get "riled up inside."

2. **The Supervisor should make himself available** so that his employees can express themselves when things bother them. He should, in other words, provide an open channel of communication between himself and his staff. The Supervisor who is always too busy to see or hear from his subordinates provides the most fertile ground for the growth of grievances.

3. **The Supervisor should inquire frequently how things are going** or whether anything is bothering the employee. He should keep his eyes open and watch for signs of discontent that may not be expressed directly by the employee concerned.

4. **The Supervisor should explain changes.** One of the greatest causes for complaint and discontent is change. Changing anything is cause for alarm. People feel secure in knowing and doing the same thing on a regular basis, and change frightens them. But if changes are explained in advance and the employee is properly motivated,

there is a good chance he will take them in his stride.

Despite all good intentions and efforts to prevent complaints from developing, the Supervisor will not always succeed, and he may be confronted with a full-blown grievance to deal with. The student may wonder why there is such concern. So there is a grievance? So what? This is the time and place then to discuss the seriousness of grievances insofar as the Supervisor, and especially the new or young Supervisor, is concerned.

Let us visualize the following scene: Daisy Scott confronts her Department Head, Diana Sloane. "Miss Sloane, I have been trying to see you all week about something that is bothering me, but you have been either too busy or not available. I must talk to you now or I'm going up to the Personnel Department and ask for a transfer or resign, or something! Or: "Miss Sloane, unless you listen to what is bothering me and try to straighten things out, you will force me to go see Mr. Phillips, the Merchandise Manager. I'm sure he will get things moving around here."

In any case, the important fact remains that no first-line Supervisor wants *his* superior to be called in, directly or indirectly, to poke around and uncover little things that he may have neglected or been too busy to do. In other words, the Department Head does well to avoid washing any of his dirty linen in public. If a grievance is presented to him, the Supervisor should do the following:

1. Listen!

    a. Insure complete privacy so the employee can air his grievance.

    b. Put the employee at ease.

c. Be courteous.

   d. Give the employee all the time he needs — don't rush him.

   e. Listen patiently, attentively, and without prejudice or interruption.

   f. Be sure to inform the employee *when* he can expect an answer — don't just say: "I'll let you know."

2. **Look!**

   a. Examine all the facts.

   b. Investigate. There are more than two sides to a story, so look at the problem from all angles.

   c. Get the opinion of others, if necessary. Perhaps a fellow Supervisor can be helpful if he has had a similar problem.

   d. Decide whether you need help (from your superior or from the Personnel Department) or will handle this grievance yourself.

   e. Consider alternative solutions. Consider what effect your preferred solution will have, not only on the employee(s) concerned, but on your department as a whole.

3. **Stop!**

   a. Come to a definite decision — one which you feel should end the grievance.

- **b.** Solve the grievance by acting promptly but not hastily.

- **c.** Inform the employee of your decision.

- **d.** If you were unable to do anything to really help the employee, be sure that he knows all the alternative solutions you considered but were forced to discard for good reasons.

- **e.** If you have a solution, put it in motion and follow it up to determine to what extent you have resolved the grievance.

- **f.** If your preferred solution did not work out, as indicated by your follow-up, put your alternative solution into action and follow it up as well.

The Supervisor holds the key to solving grievances, as indicated in the outline above. The Supervisor must be able not only to solve grievances, but to prevent them from reaching that state by recognizing them when they are minor complaints. The Supervisor must learn to eliminate as many of the causes of complaints as possible and to handle those that remain as effectively and as soon as he is able.

Recommended Reading

Dooher and Marquis: Effective Communication on the Job — pp. 195-210

Ecker, MacRae et al: Handbook for Supervisors — Chapter 13

Flippo: Principles of Personnel Management — pp. 437-439, 444-447

Chapter Eighteen

The Supervisor and Frequent, Long-Range Problems

The conclusion of this manual for the Workshop in Executive Leadership will be a discussion of some frequent and long-range problems that will constantly confront the Supervisor. While there are many more such problems than we have time to cover here, we have selected the following:

1. Rumors
2. Absenteeism
3. Familiarity and Fraternization
4. Collections
5. Alcoholism on the Job
6. The Older Worker

RUMORS

All democratic countries pride themselves on freedom of speech – one of the basic rights of the individual. The highest courts in the land have, however, ruled that this fundamental concept has its limitations. For example, freedom of speech does not permit an individual to yell "Fire" in a crowded place; that could cause panic, a stampede, and might result in many deaths. This limitation must also be applied to freedom of speech in the business world.

The Supervisor can do little to discourage his subordinates from talking among themselves. But *what* they are saying can seriously jeopardize the moral of his department and/or the entire firm. And yet it is quite obvious that talk among employees cannot be abolished or even suppressed. We are all familiar with the iron discipline that prevails in our prison systems as portrayed in movies and on television. Even in such a controlled environment, nothing can be done to eliminate the spreading of rumors. The prison grapevine operates quietly and efficiently, in spite of the strictest controls.

It is imperative that the Supervisor be equipped to recognize the dangers of rumor spreading and be able to deal effectively with the problem. If employees *will* talk, then it is important for the Supervisor to know (1) *what* they are saying, (2) *how* the rumors are spreading, (3) *why* rumors spread, and (4) *what can be done* about rumors.

What are Employees Talking About?

The grapevine, as rumor spreading is popularly called, is usually of two distinct types or forms:

1. Gossiping or scandal mongering is the nasty

reputation-destroying form of rumor spreading that is part of all levels of society, as well as business. Some people are malicious gossips, while others merely enjoy listening to and passing on a juicy morsel about a fellow employee or Supervisor.

2. **Rumors concerning the business** can have a very negative effect on the morale of employees and play havoc with production or sales. When misinformation, which most rumors are, is spread about the company's present policies, future plans, etc., it can destroy much of the good will management has established between itself and its employees.

How Rumors Spread

Studies by industrial psychologists and behavioral science experts on the "science" of rumor spreading have uncovered some interesting facts about this phenomena in business. They reveal that most workers do not spread rumors, but act as passive receivers of such information. While most workers enjoy being "in" on such items, there are only a handful of chronic gossips who are constantly transmitting rumors or stimulating ideas to pass on to the receivers of gossip or rumor.

Why Rumors?

The psychological studies previously mentioned have also provided the answer to the most fundamental question of all: Why are rumors spread? Essentially, it goes back to the basic drive for security by most individuals on the job. The rumor spreaders are seeking the recognition that comes when they start something going; everyone looks up to them as leaders or as knowledgeable people. Those who receive or pass such information, do so in seeking to know more about something that may affect their economic life — again a form of insecurity.

In their search for greater security, employees very often spread rumors resulting in widespread insecurity. Some frequent topics for rumors that lead to feelings of insecurity are: automation, adoption of self-service sales methods, the closing of a branch, plant, or store, etc. Rumors concerning absorption by conglomerates which will cause consolidations and layoffs, and rumors about raises or bonuses that will probably never materialize can circulate and cause panic, despair, and have a very negative effect on morale.

What Can Be Done About Rumors?

In the case of the gossipper or scandal monger, where the rumor is damaging the reputation of an individual, the problem can frequently be solved by the Supervisor taking disciplinary action against those responsible.

But in the case of the busy grapevine involving business activities, the Supervisor himself may be partially responsible for the rumor. The fact is that many rumors start as a result of poor communications between the Supervisor and his staff, sometimes a complete breakdown resulting from workers' questions which the Supervisor can't or won't answer. When employees meet such a lack of communication, they turn to the grapevine, which is only too available to take up the Supervisor's task and distort the real facts more and more as the rumor spreads further and further from its source.

It is the Supervisor's responsibility, therefore, to keep his staff informed by keeping *himself* well-informed. When he gets information, he should and must pass it on to his subordinates. The employee must get the *facts*, all of them, or as much information as possible if rumor spreading is to be stopped or prevented. Once the facts have been supplied, the vacuum within the rumor causes it to disappear.

ABSENTEEISM

It is quite obvious that no matter what the Supervisor may do, there will always be a relative amount of absenteeism in any department or firm. But the Supervisor has a big stake in the employee's attendance records. If the Supervisor is "getting work done through people," then the people must be there *regularly* to get this work done. Otherwise production (sales) will suffer, schedules must be juggled, and all sorts of problems can and do arise. Of course, the cost to the firm, if sick leave is involved, must also be reckoned with.

Why Absenteeism?

Despite the intangibility of this problem, research has revealed and experience has confirmed that there are a number of reasons that reappear regularly as a cause for frequent absence:

1. The common cold causes at least half of all absences.

2. The larger the company, the greater the tendency for absenteeism. The employees of smaller companies feel closer to the "top," whereas in the larger firm, the employee feels lost in numbers and does not have the same feeling of loyalty to the Supervisor or the firm.

3. The number of people absent is probably quite high the day before and/or the day after a holiday; this is also true over the week-end — Monday is the highest absentee day in the business world.

4. Where a higher female-absentee rate exists, look for deeper causes than simple sexual discrimination: Are the women

employees *treated* as inferiors? Are the women employees given the same opportunities for advancement as the men? Are the women employees' salaries on a par with the men's?

5. There is a direct relationship between good supervision and absenteeism. Several important studies have left little doubt that the lowest absence record groups were those who liked their jobs and felt that their Supervisors were treating them right.

What Can Be Done About Absenteeism?

If the alert Supervisor wishes to do something about absenteeism, he must first convince himself that a good attendance record is important; then he will have an easy time convincing his staff that they should be similarly concerned. Too frequently, the Supervisor just duly notes that an employee is absent. The Supervisor needs to know *why* and *how often* and *when* the absences occur; a real stretch of illness, etc., can be discounted; but only real attention can reveal a long-term sporadic absenteeism. Getting onto absenteeism early — in the first six months to a year of the employee's tenure — can cure it by a series of heart-to-heart talks, reprimands or probation. Once the word gets around that the Supervisor is interested in *all* absences and wants to know the *reason* for each of them, there will be a natural lessening in absences by all of the rank and file.

FAMILIARITY AND FRATERNIZATION

The question of how friendly the Supervisor should be with those who come under his supervision has long been with us; but this presents even greater problems to the young Supervisor. Trained under the prevalent philosophy of human relations, imbued with the spirit of democracy-in-business, and believing that friendliness is an important trait of the good Supervisor, the new breed of Supervisor is truly perplexed by the question: "How friendly should you be? Where does friendliness end and over-familiarity and fraternization begin?"

The problem may be conveniently divided into three parts:

1. How should the Supervisor be addressed?

2. Should the Supervisor become obligated to his subordinates?

3. The case against socialization or fraternization.

Addressing the Supervisor

What should the rank and file call the Supervisor? How should they address him? Similarly, how should the Supervisor, particularly the new Supervisor, address the employees under his supervision? First, let's look at both the right way and the wrong way for a Supervisor to address an employee.

Miss Doris Brown, Supervisor, addressing Miss Rose Smith, salesperson:

Right:

> "Miss Smith, please give me a count of those Lady Manhattan blouses."

Wrong:

> "Rose, please give me a count of those Lady Manhattan blouses."

Now, let's look at the proper form of address when the employee communicates with the Supervisor.

Miss Rose Smith, salesperson, addressing Miss Doris Brown, Supervisor:

Right:

> "Miss Brown, may I take my lunch hour at 11:30 today?"

Wrong:

> "Say, Doris, may I take my lunch hour at 11:30 today?"

From the above, it is obvious that the writer belongs to the "old school" — he is opposed to Supervisor-employee relations which put them on a "first name" basis. This is especially true when "the public" is present or within earshot. The use of first names (and even worse, nicknames) is the first step toward lowering the bars of respect and restraint that are required for proper employee-employer relationships. It breeds familiarity and gives the employee a feeling that he can be free and easy in all aspects of his relationship with his boss.

Of course, it can very well be that the first-line Supervisor will not have any choice in this matter. If *his* Supervisor, a middle-management person, or even a top management executive sets the policy of a "first name" basis, the young Supervisor must follow suit, albeit reluctantly.

Becoming Obligated

Another pitfall to be avoided by the Supervisor is becoming

obligated to members of his staff. The Supervisor should never borrow money, or ask members of his department to buy him things or do him favors of any kind. It is difficult for the Supervisor to discipline an employee, for example, if he owes him "$20 until pay day."

Socialization

The third obstacle that the friendly Supervisor must hurdle is a big one: how to resist the temptation of being "one of the boys." This problem can take many forms, such as:

    a. "Miss Davis (Supervisor), the girls are meeting at 6 p.m. at Bill's Bar on the corner for an informal "happy hour"; won't you join us for a leisurely drink or two?"

    b. "Mr. Black (Department Head), John Kent is buying a block of tickets to the new musical that got such rave notices; shall we get you two tickets, too?"

    c. "Miss Brody (Department Manager), the girls of our department take turns in being hostess to a monthly party at home. We would like you to come and bring an escort this Saturday night at Rhoda Levine's house."

    d. "Mr. Bruce (Supervisor), would you like to join the boys at our regular Wednesday evening bowling night?"

    e. "Miss Telford (assistant buyer), some of the girls are going to dinner and then to a movie; we do this quite regularly – would you like to join us tonight?"

These are but a few of the many possible socializing opportunities that might come the Supervisor's way. Again the spectre arises: how do you discipline the employee you danced with the night before? The author feels that the Supervisor must turn down all such invitations, tempting as they may be. Of course, the important, once-in-a-lifetime invitations such as weddings, christenings, etc. (and even funerals) should be accepted, if possible. An employee will feel honored by the Supervisor's presence.

Most employees do not expect their bosses to be "hail fellows well met". They generally don't look for a drinking partner, so the necessity to work at being sociable is really not present. The average worker wants someone he can respect as a Supervisor because of his management ability, not his fraternizing graces.

COLLECTIONS

A minor but frequently annoying and painful problem is the matter of taking up collections for various and sundry persons, charities, and drives. In some departments it seems that hardly a day or a week goes by without somebody collecting something for someone. Sometimes the cause is worthy; at other times it can be a real nuisance. In addition to these intradepartment collections, there are, of course, the annual drives of the standard, charitable organizations such as the Red Cross, Salvation Army, Red Feather Community Fund, etc., most of which are company-supported or sponsored. To these "worthy" causes may be added the favorite charities of various individuals of the department, such as heart funds, cancer drives, etc. These are usually solicited for by the most aggressive members of the department, all intent on making a good showing for their pet charity.

On top of all this charitable endeavor is the normal collection-making that takes place in any department for such events as birthdays, engagements, retirements, illness, deaths, marriages, leave-takings, etc. Accordingly, experience has shown that the Supervisor must take a firm hand in controlling the collection problem. The alert Supervisor will inform his department that all collections *must* adhere to the following regulations:

1. All collections of all kinds must have the approval of the Department Head (preferably in writing), who should examine the reasons for the collection carefully before giving permission.

2. Whenever possible, an amount must not be mentioned to the donor — the employees should be free to give what they can or wish.

3. Soliciting must not interfere with the department's normal operation.

4. All collecting must be done individually and absolutely privately. Under no circumstances should the Supervisor permit solicitation of anyone in another's presence.

5. If the employee has or had little or no contact with the person for whom the collection is being made, he should not be approached for a donation at all.

6. No one should feel he must give unless he really wants to — no pressure should be permitted.

7. Supervisors should *never* make collections for any reason. It goes without saying that such soliciting has the distinct aroma of: "give or else."

Once the department membership knows that the Supervisor means business by promulgating rules such as the above, the disagreeable aspects of collections will gradually disappear. This is especially true if the Supervisor insists that gifts be uniform and given to all on an equal basis.

One way to enforce this rule of equality and impartiality is to establish a "Sunshine" or "Cheer" fund. By means of regular, small, voluntary monetary collections, the Supervisor can see the department build up a sizeable "Kitty." From such a fund, gifts are made for all notable and worthy occasions on an equal basis. Thus a wedding present will not vary from person to person nor will the size of the floral tribute increase or diminish on the occasion of a funeral.

ALCOHOLISM

Generally speaking, except for a few of the nation's largest industrial organizations, the alcholic, particularly one who has reached the stage of being compelled to drink on the job, has only one fate — dismissal. A relatively small number of firms, sometimes in conjunction with a union, have attempted to treat the alcoholic as the sick person he is. But the overwhelming cases of drinking on the job end up as disciplinary cases with dismissal rightfully a foregone conclusion. The Supervisor has the painful duty to root out the chronic drinker and dismiss him as soon as possible, unless there is a rehabilitation program available and sanctioned by the company.

There are a number of obvious reasons for this seemingly "tough" attitude. If the alcoholic injures or kills himself on the job and his family or estate institutes a large-sized negligence lawsuit, the Supervisor is sure to be made a direct party to the suit. This is equally true if the alcoholic's actions or negligence causes injury or death to a co-worker or customer. The Supervisor puts his entire career on the line by not exposing the drinker as soon as possible. Top Management will consider the Supervisor neither alert nor intelligent, and even downright negligent, should he fail to seek out the alcoholic and prevent any trouble he may cause. It is very important, therefore, for the Supervisor to be able to recognize the alcoholic on the job.

Some clues to such a recognition follow:

1. Physical symptoms, while not always entirely accurate, can be helpful in making an initial determination, particularly the "hangover" syndrome — bloodshot eyes, red flushed face, hand tremors, and a foul alcoholic breath that defies disguise by mints and breath cleansers.

2. The workday schedule of the chronic drinker can be easily recognized:

    a. A quick drink before work (or at coffee break — before 10 a.m.).

    b. Downslide before lunch — low ebb of the morning.

    c. Recovery during lunch. (Did he "drink his lunch"? You bet he did.)

    d. Downhill again before the afternoon break — if any.

    e. If able to refresh during afternoon, all is well.

    f. If no opportunity, low ebb all afternoon to quitting time.

g. Always home late — an hour or two after work.

h. All set for the evening.

i. Low point before going home.

j. And so to bed.

3. The behavior patterns on a number of fronts are remarkably clear:

a. Frequent absences, particularly on Mondays, but also a bad attendance record in general, including taking off part of the day (because they could not be without drinking for such a long time).

b. Use of excuses, including all sorts of minor illnesses, later on developing into other fantastic stories which get progressively more unbelievable.

c. At social functions they outdrink everyone else, but they want others to join them as a "cover up."

d. Behavior away from the job tends to involve domestic trouble, money problems, and sometimes disorderly conduct, resulting in police action.

Since alcoholism is an emotional disorder, the Supervisor would do well to avoid playing the amateur psychiatrist. It is enough for the Supervisor to recognize the alcoholic on the job and to get rid of him before anyone gets hurt.

OLDER WORKERS

The young Supervisor, especially the relatively new Department Head, will frequently find supervising people older than himself a trial. The problem may be solely because of the age difference between the younger Supervisor and the older worker, or it may be unrelated to age but masked by it. For example, an employee may feel rejected that he or she was not chosen to be Supervisor and therefore may decide to downgrade everything the "young newcomer" does; thus the real problem—resentment—is masked by the age difference. Or an older employee may feel that he or she "knows better"—not just better than younger people, but better than everyone—and therefore may decide to continue doing things just the way he or she did in the past, regardless of what the "young newcomer" says to do; thus the real problem—egotism—is masked by the age difference.

Or the problem may be, of course, solely because of the age difference: solely because of a younger person's inability to adopt a realistic attitude toward older people, or on the other hand, solely because of an older person's inability to listen objectively to, and to take instructions from, a younger Supervisor.

Whatever the problem, however, the first step is to define it. Is it legitimately a problem caused by the age difference between a Supervisor and a worker, or is this merely masking the real underlying problem?

Analyze the problem carefully, making especially sure that the problem is not because of *your* attitude. Try to understand the "other guy" better, so that you can define the problem and therefore work at its solution. Use diplomacy in your communications with older employees; for example, make it clear that you fully understand that someone with years' experience is a very valuable source of help, that you respect the ideas of others, that you plan to work harmoniously with all other workers, that you intend to listen as well as to instruct, that you see no age barrier among workers, and so on. Well-applied psychology in many instances will turn negative workers, older *and* younger, to *your* side.

Recommended Reading

A.M.A.: Leadership on the Job — pp. 85-93, 259-261, 206-209, 224-231

Dooher and Marquis: Effective Communication on the Job — pp. 116-122

Halsey, George D.: Supervising People — Chapter 17

A final word . . .

A supervisor's job is to plan and supervise the work of others, to think for more than one, to multiply himself through others. He puts first things first and makes decisions promptly and clearly when problems arise. He is primarily a teacher and a leader, who directs, with personal touch, inspiring energetic loyalty. He shows workers how to do things easily, better, at less cost. He goes to his subordinates to make suggestions, express appreciation, get information. He invites them to confer with him and be perfectly at ease, then encouranges enthusiasm, initiative, thinking, and is receptive to new ideas whatever their source. He gives clear-cut instructions, and delegates authority with responsibility. He trains those under him to think and decide for themselves; he avoids giving assignments beyond recipients' capacity to execute. He is paid for what he gets done as well as for what he does. A supervisor is "good" to the extent of his ability to recognize, accept and act upon good advice. When wrong he admits it, thereby grows in the eyes of his associates and others. His most prized possession is judgment and judgment is the faculty for making right decisions most of the time. A supervisor demands respect by giving respect to his fellow worker regardless of position. A supervisor above all must learn . . . *You can't do it alone!*

Good Luck!

Bibliography

Bibliography

Beach, Dale S.: *Personnel: The Management of People at Work.* The MacMillan Co., New York.

Beckman, R. O.: *How To Train Supervisors.* Harper & Brothers, New York.

Craig, Robert L. & Bittel, Lester R.: *Training and Development Handbook.* McGraw Hill Book Co., New York.

Dooher, Joseph M. & Marquis, Vivienne: *The Development of Executive Talent.* American Management Association, New York.

Dooher, Joseph M. & Marquis, Vivienne: *Effective Communication on The Job.* American Management Association, New York.

Ecker, Paul; Macrae, John; Oulette, Vernon; and Telford, Charles: *Handbook for Supervisors.* Prentice-Hall, Englewood Cliffs, New Jersey.

Famularo, Joseph J.: *Supervisors in Action.* McGraw Hill Book Company, New York.

Flippo, Edwin B.: *Principles of Personnel Management.* McGraw Hill Book Company, New York.

Halsey, George D.: *Selecting and Developing First-Line Supervisors.* Harper & Brothers, New York.

Halsey, George D.: *Training Employees.* Harper & Brothers, New York.

Lipsett, Laurence; Rogers, Frank P.; and Kentner, Harold M.: *Personnel Selection and Recruitment.* Allyn & Bacon, Boston.

Pfiffner, John M. & Fels, Marshall: *The Supervision of Personnel.* Prentice-Hall, Englewood Cliffs, New Jersey.

Sartain, Aaron Q. & Baker, Alton W.: *The Supervisor and His Job.* McGraw Hill Book Company, New York.

Sayles, Leonard R. & Strauss, George: *Human Behavior in Organization.* Prentice-Hall, Englewood Cliffs, New Jersey.

Straus, George & Sayles, Leonard R: *Personnel: The Human Problems of Management.* Prentice-Hall, Englewood Cliffs, New Jersey.

BOBBS-MERRILL EDUCATIONAL PUBLISHING
Fashion Merchandising Series

Color, Line, and Design

Executive Leadership

Fashion Buying

Fashion Sales Promotion

Fashion Coordination

Fashion Textiles and Laboratory Workbook
   (with Fashion Textile Kit)

Fashion Vocabulary and Dictation

Fashion Writing

Internship Program Workbook

Principles of Personal Selling

Selected Cases in Fashion Marketing (*2 Volumes*)

Techniques of Fashion Merchandising